Movement Of Stillness

As Revealed In The New Mayan Calendar-Post 2012

- Channeled prophecies from Edgar Cayce
- Visual design of the new Mayan calendar
- Crystal messages of Higher Truths

Jacqui Derbecker

BALBOA.
PRESS
A DIVISION OF HAY HOUSE

Balboa Press books may be ordered through booksellers or by contacting:

Balboa Press
A Division of Hay House
1663 Liberty Drive
Bloomington, IN 47403
www.balboapress.com
1-(877) 407-4847

Because of the dynamic nature of the Internet, any web addresses or
links contained in this book may have changed since publication and
may no longer be valid. The views expressed in this work are solely those
of the author and do not necessarily reflect the views of the publisher,
and the publisher hereby disclaims any responsibility for them.

The author of this book does not dispense medical advice or prescribe the use
of any technique as a form of treatment for physical, emotional, or medical
problems without the advice of a physician, either directly or indirectly. The
intent of the author is only to offer information of a general nature to help you
in your quest for emotional and spiritual well-being. In the event you use any
of the information in this book for yourself, which is your constitutional right,
the author and the publisher assume no responsibility for your actions.

Any people depicted in stock imagery provided by Thinkstock are models,
and such images are being used for illustrative purposes only.
Certain stock imagery © Thinkstock.

ISBN: 978-1-4525-3708-5 (e)
ISBN: 978-1-4525-3707-8 (sc)

Printed in the United States of America

Balboa Press rev. date: 11/8/2011

"Seeing beauty in a flower can awaken you, however, briefly, to the beauty that is an essential part of your own innermost being, your true nature . . ."

ECKHART TOLLE

"Spirit gives life, and everyone on this planet has Spirit within them as an all-powerful force for good . . ."

DR. WAYNE DYER

"Can you coax your mind from wandering and keep the original oneness?"

BYRON KATIE

"We see the world piece by piece, as the sun, the moon, the animal, the tree; but the whole, of which these are the shining parts, is the soul."

RALPH WALDO EMMERSON

Gifted To You . . .
And the Divine within Yourself

Contents

Acknowledgements

First and foremost I wish to give an abundance of love and gratitude to Spirit/White Light. It is also with great joy that I make the following acknowledgements.

For the caring and support of my heart family: Marly Freer, Sandra Fetch, Jill Strapp, Suzanne Dobinson, Sarah Beveridge, Cheryl McCague-Shane, Jocelyn Griffiths, Colleen Noseworthy, Lona McBoyle, Pat O'Connor, Briar Galloway, and John Teffer for your generous contribution. For the timeless typing efforts of Shannon Chan – you are amazing. Thank you to the wonderful Mary Ellen Koroscil for your unending editing, and to the Balboa team for your guidance in piecing these channeled messages together. A very special thank-you to all of the evening participants at The Waterview Space.

Acknowledgements and thanks to the voices of those teachers quoted herein. Finally, I want to thank the late Edgar Cayce for his presence in my life. It has been a great honor to be a vessel for his message to move through me to you. I am grateful.

Synchronicities happen every single millisecond of the day, not just once in a while.

Part 1

The Beginning Messages

Introduction

This book contains messages that have just simply streamed or channeled through me. I have been engaged in a process of what is described as *automatic writing*, where messages move through me via my handwriting.

It began for me several years ago on my thirty-seventh birthday. I was writing in my journal and all at once felt a warmth expand from inside of me and near me. I then began to write but without any effort or thinking. The words or messages fell from my pen onto the paper as if someone else were controlling my hand. The feelings were peace*full*, joy, and a knowing that I was a vessel for the messages to move through me from Spirit. That was over ten years ago and large stacks of handwritten sheets later.

Spirits that communicate through me using automatic writing or channeling are now speaking to me by my voice. In other words, instead of simply writing messages I am now honored to speak with Spirit verbally. I knew that I have been given an opportunity to help others through these abilities. I assist others through one-to-one sessions by communicating with Spirit and their guides. I also present topic-specific channeled messages to large groups of people.

I am not special; I just show up and allow the messages to move through me either verbally or written. Opening my heart and just allowing the words to flow is my only job.

This particular book is a channeled message as streamlined from Spirit and Edgar Cayce through me. Edgar Cayce (1877–1945) was a well-known mystic philosopher and medical intuitive. Cayce tapped into the wisdom of the unconscious mind. He provided fascinating anecdotal evidence of the success of medical perspective readings. His other work focused on spiritual growth, ancient civilizations, reincarnation, life purpose, and issues of integrating body, mind, and Spirit into daily life. He is actually regarded as the creator of the body, mind, and soul connection to healing. Cayce was therefore a channeler, a seer, and a medium. Several books about his work have been published, one named *Edgar Cayce: My Life as a Seer* (Cayce, Edgar. *My Life as a Seer.* New York, NY. St. Martin's. 1997.) It was a great honor for me to channel or transmit his messages. As a result this entire book is comprised of hundreds of automatically hand written pads of paper.

The messages within this book contain the Mayan calendar post-2012 prophecies or now-named "All Truths." In fact, prophecies or All Truths were at one point in time called the mystic laws. There are approximately one hundred of these All Truths described in great detail within this book. They each touch upon the living aspects of career, emotion, finance, physical body, mind, Spirit, community, and relationship. You will notice that some of the channeled words have changed their spelling and form in order to enrich the context. As well as the terms God, Source, and White Light are used interchangeably. It doesn't really matter what term you use to signify the One Creator. You will notice a repetition of certain words and phrases. This is done purposefully in order to bring forth and emphasize the beauty of the energy or feelings of these words intermingled within this book.

I invite you to read and feel the language of these messages as channeled for you. As you explore the messages within these pages, you will notice a gentle building of the energy and information as it is presented to you. In other words, the further you delve into the reading, the more energy intense it becomes, and yet at the same time it is *freeing*.

It is freeing like the butterfly as it floats along its path. These beautiful, graceful creatures find indomitable will from their inner strength to maintain their *movement of stillness*. The butterfly, an unstoppable Spirit, flies thousands of miles along its migratory path. It is unconquerable as it flutters and floats through the power of the winds. The butterfly's process is driven by the strength of its inner being. In their weakness they find this strength, which is the stillness within.

This process should not be halted. It is now time for individuals to accept the *movement of stillness* and the ushering in of the *Oneness* of 2012 and post-2012.

Poet John Teffer captures the butterfly's *movement of stillness* in his poem entitled "The Butterfly Floats," which he uniquely created for this book.

The Butterfly Floats

With its *Movement of Stillness*
The Butterfly Floats
On Time's Eternal Wings
Weathering The Wind
Undaunted by Time Or Distance
It Transcends The Unbelievable
To Transform Its Quest
To Be

Read this book over and over again. Absorb the energy that the words unveil to your Spirit. Allow the Spirit of truth to reform your being into the Oneness that is love and protection.

The Mayan Calendar

The end of the Mayan calendar *appears* to be December 21, 2012. Rest assured that you shouldn't be concerned regarding those who are convinced that the time has arrived for the end of the world or Armageddon. This type of thinking is a falsehood. The new Mayan calendar indicates there is *nothing and yet everything going on.*

Post-December 21, 2012, is a time for recognitions. In other words, it is the realization that an energetic shift is occurring around the world and the preparation for this shift is currently evolving now and beyond. This shift is energetically reshaping the planet back to its original state and is known as the *dawning of a new era.*

Beauty, peace, passion, blessings, joy, and grace will prevail upon our planet. These authentic spiritual feelings will resonate throughout the entire planet, thus creating a healing effect. People will become more aware of their soul's purpose, authentic self, and living in the *now.*

This phenomenon is actually occurring *now* on a spiritual level that can never be symbolized or recognized by the intellect (the mind). The intellect fails to understand the unending/eternal Spirit. From this day forward, the Mayan calendar is all about Spirit, indicating that post-December 21, 2012, will continue throughout eternity. Spirit is eternal, as predicted by the Mayan ancient civilization prophecy. It is neither wisdom nor knowledge. It is simply a feeling and a knowing, nothing more. *It just is.*

Post-2012 is a time of awakening. This is a time to realign one's self to live an authentic life filled with the love of who you really are. It is as simple as this. This is not a hippie-granola concept or fantasy but an era of spiritual self-exploration. This shift is presently occurring upon the planet and deep within you.

This point in time (history) was predicted or prophesized many years ago by Edgar Cayce in the twentieth century. He was a well-known mystic philosopher, medical intuitive, and channeler. His work has been published in several books, and he still remains in high regard around the world. His prophecy of this place in time is a point of reconciliation of your authentic self. This book is a gift to you and contains Edgar Cayce's predicted truths as channeled through me.

Link

As a reader, it is important for you to understand the link between Edgar Cayce and the Mayan calendar, plus the mystic laws and how this channeled process worked. I tapped into Cayce's channeled prophecies. This work is channeled information as extracted from the mystic energy of not only the Mayans but also from Spirit or White Light. It is slightly more complex than this, but the link between Cayce and the Mayan calendar and the mystic laws stem from *crystallized messages*. A detailed explanation of this link through the crystallized messages and what they entail will be fully explained in subsequent chapters of this book.

The explanation will evolve through the description and the *visual design of the new Mayan calendar, post-December 21, 2012.* The Mayans created the calendar through a channeled system and this is what Edgar Cayce tapped into. Currently, this is the basis for information being revealed to you in this book as I streamed into Cayce's channeled messages.

It has been my honor to birth these messages. Clarity of this channeled work will present itself to you as you read further. I'd like to explain and provide some insights to you as to how this book was birthed.

I isolated myself in a fabulous art/yoga center nestled among the mountains in New Mexico. The serenity of the atmosphere created the calm energy that I required to focus upon the messages moving through me. The center had no radios, televisions, cell phones, and very limited Internet access. Therefore the electrical buzzing was minimal – perfect conditions to channel. I awoke every morning at 3:00 a.m. and channeled six to eight hours a day for a total of six weeks.

When living in this stream of channeling, for hours on end I simply insulate myself. I tend not to expend any form of energy except for the messages gifting through me. I clear my thoughts, allowing myself to be an open vessel. Within this *zone* I am best able to accomplish the process of channeling. As messages flow through me, my hand moves in an automatic continuous fashion. There is no time to think or edit any language; it is a steady flow of information. I am unaware of what is streaming through me onto the paper until it's complete.

During the channeling process I eat very lightly and specifically, and my menu consists mainly of fruits, vegetables and plenty of lemon water. When residing at the center, the chef would prepare for me a vegetarian meal free of gluten, sugar, dairy, meat, alcohol, and caffeine. When one channels, it is important to have one's mind and body clear. Certain foods create blockages that tend to clog the deeper messages that wish to transmit through you.

At the art/yoga center I finalized the core work of Edgar Cayce's channeled messages. It was here where I tapped into the pages of this book and I could distinctly hear Cayce's voice as he read to me. It was an amazing experience. With my EasyWrite pen and pads of lined paper, I handwrote for several hours each day, refraining from using a computer as the electrical waves seem to influence the channeling system. I was open to receiving Cayce's messages captured within these pages. I was simply his vessel. In fact, his Spirit is very much with us today.

When I completed channeling this book, I literally felt like I had birthed something incredible. I required several days to sleep and rest. And yet after completing hundreds of channeled handwritten pages, I felt a heightened sense of purpose.

There were close to one hundred prophecies (now known as All Truths) pertaining to 2012 and post-2012 that streamed through me. These All Truths contained in this book were created from the mystic laws.

The All Truths that I channeled simply state, "You are the Source/White Light – nothing more." During this time in history, you will begin to feel spiritual shifts and start to recognize that everything is in a perfect plan of order. You will come to the realization that something profound is at work here. The Mayans have always predicted this shift or *dawning of the new Age of Aquarius in our original world*. They declare this truth, defined as "living in Spirit" and nothing more.

The end of the old Mayan calendar as perceived by intellects, ones who study Mayan symbols, perhaps, haven't come to the realization that now is the time for Spirit to make itself completely known. You are no doubt curious as to how living in Spirit will occur. It is not through intellectual wisdom or knowledge.

Living in Spirit is through hope, love, dignity, passion, compassion, peace, and an elegance of grace. This type of information is being shared at an enormous rate around the world. More and more people are recognizing they are already enlightened. Individuals are keen to learn about living one's soul's purpose and discovering how to live an authentic life.

Numerous discussions are occurring regarding the subject of ego and how this ego loves to consume and ply on the suffering of oneself. These discussions involve learning how to dissolve or dismantle the ego from one's self *(ego* meaning "*e*dging *g*race *o*ut)."

I believe that you can begin to realize what is transpiring *now.* There is a knowing *shift* within the Spirit of each person. This shift is slowly nudging each person back to his or her original self or to the original world, which is the core belief of the message of the new Mayan calendar.

There is a dramatic change in the *now* type of existence which can change your way of being. There are young children, adolescents, and young adults who are receiving the message and acting on it. Today there are many children being born who are Star children, Indigo children, Rainbow children, Atlantis/ Crystal children, and others. These children may be considered to be psychic kids – they feel, sense, touch, hear, and see angels, Spirits of nature, and more. Personally, within my consulting practice, I have met children who have recognized their psychic abilities as early as three years of age. Actually all people have psychic abilities, you just need to bring awareness to yourself from within. Children may be extremely sensitive. It remains vital that they are believed and cherished by their parents/ guardians. They must be nurtured and provided with love and attention. It is also important that they meet other Spirit-like children in order to feel that they are okay. They may feel different or out of place or even lonely. In addition, parents of children with psychic-ability awareness need to be taught how to effectively deal with their children. This phenomenon will have far-reaching effects, particularly in the therapeutic field. Perhaps a misdiagnosis of our children who have psychic abilities is occurring?

The future within my practice includes long-range plans to establish a registry for children. This community connection would be most valuable for children who have the awareness of their psychic abilities and for their families.

Furthermore, you will also see adolescents and young adults who hold a very strong sense of the world of Spirit. They are here to assist in this age of paradigm shifting toward Spirit.

It's important to realize that the children/adolescents/young adults are not here to speak about ego, war, injury, punishment, doubt, and material wealth. They are all here to speak about light, love, peace, passion, joy, and compassion and to help others to recognize Spirit within themselves. You might say that they are here to convey a positive message about embracing our spiritual selves.

This shift to the realization of total acceptance of who you are is the core prophecy of 2012 and post-2012. The prophecies or All Truths are outlined in complete detail via these pages. I invite you to listen to who you are and be prepared to arrive in this particular place of *stay*. You can seamlessly move into this home of Spirit, which is recognized and realized by a multitude of people. When you are in this state, you will be awakened by glorious ideas, thoughts, feelings, and opinions. It is within this state of *bliss* or *awakened* awareness that you realize that nothing else matters.

At this point in time all answers of Spirit are available. While living in this bliss-filled, awakened state, savor the moments of beauty found in the contents of 2012 and beyond. You will get it! Here it is: simply become familiar and accustomed to the inner sacred place of who you are. When you arrive at this realization, you then live within the realm of who you really are. Then and only then will you realize what is transpiring. There will be readjustments to the fact that nothing else matters except for life and Spirit itself.

There is actually a silence generated from within oneself called the *knowing, the Oneness of self,* the entirety of existence – the completeness of who you are. As you move forward in your life, you can live from this inner sacred place of stillness. You will learn to reside within the inner meaning of knowing, an inner Oneness.

As you awaken to the fact that you are Spirit first and human second, then everything around you and within you changes or transitions. You become filled with the excitement of being a new you. It is the part of you that really is you or your *original self* or *Essence.* This is your knowing realization, a way of being. It is the way all things exist in this world.

We are now in a time of recognition or awakening of self, where all people are realizing there is more to life. "There has to be more meaning to life," you hear people say. "There just must be more!" This thought is in fact the beginning of the transitioning or the shifting into a new way of thinking, which is your original self, meaning Spirit. This is the message of 2012 and post-2012. It is a complete change into living a more conscious way of being. Every millisecond of the *now* shifts are happening, and it's an exciting era.

This *now* time has been perfectly planned and predicted by ancient civilizations hundreds and perhaps thousands of years ago. It's an era when everything becomes dismantled that is formed from ego. *Everything.* The Spirit is now making itself known through each human through an awakened state.

By *awakened* meaning, you realize who you really are. It's fascinating when one begins one's journey to an awakened lifestyle. People begin to realize that thoughts of suffering, pain, and self-sabotage are untrue. This mind-set filled with self-doubt and not being good enough, lack of confidence, and low self-esteem are also false beliefs. Perhaps you were programmed as a young child that you were not smart enough, strong enough, pretty enough, tall enough, etc., and you still are believing these old programs. Now perhaps you have added more false belief programs to your repertoire. When you awaken to the truth that you are Spirit first and human form second, then all of these false beliefs melt away. This revelation will occur as you awaken to your Spirit. You are Spirit trying to determine how to live in this human form.

Therefore the old programmed thoughts or false beliefs will reveal themselves to you as you move through your day in an awakened state. Only now can you come to the realization how every single aspect of your life has been perfectly planned.

In past history discussions concerning soul's purpose, authentic self, awakening, and Oneness were not emphasized. This Oneness is growing and gaining momentum until now there's an intensity of information that continues to manifest itself. A glimpse into the *possible* future (beyond) provides a most astounding world filled with hope and promise. There may be confusion arising from this shift for some people as they may refuse to recognize they are Spirit. Once they realize they are Spirit first, they too will shift into their authentic self.

As a result, this point in time represents a Newness of Being. This original self stems from the original world. Your old original self is your original Spirit. Spirit is first and body form is secondary. Many individuals are awakening to this truth. So remain true within yourself and you will recognize the message of the miracles in your life. These miracles are realizations of who you really are. They will surface from a genuine heartfelt place as you travel upon your life's path.

As you absorb the teachings of this book, you will notice that every word has been specifically placed in proper context of message. Each channeled message has been woven in a specific pattern that acts as a common thread throughout each chapter. This thread connects all of the pieces of the new Mayan calendar as explored within the pages of this book. Imagine a butterfly carrying a golden thread. Which is borrowed from the web of life to weave a silk cloth that dresses the new form of your Spirit.

The Divine within Yourself

As the 2012 and *post-* years approach, you may begin to connect with *your* inner world or the core of who you really are by acknowledging you are simply *The Divine*. It becomes extremely important for you to recognize who you really are: a Divine creature. This is defined as your "inner stillness." It is so vast that it has almost created a solid mass or form of matter that is designed to hold you steady and straight. This holding pattern remains to be felt and seen as only that which you truly are – "a Spirit of peace or solidity of peace" within a form named human. This Spirit is your original self.

What exactly is the meaning of all of this for each person from now until the perceived end of 2012 and post-2012? It means the core of each human is the Divine. The Divine is coming through powerfully and in greatness of being or intensity. People who are awakening to who they truly are, which is Spirit in human form, are receiving their awakened calling or they are becoming self realized. They have awakened to the realization that they are already enlightened. They are already where they need to be in life in order to receive, learn and understand who they are.

These individuals are actually feeling their Essence, which is the *solidity of stillness*. In its simplest terms, there's no need to enroll in a course or move to an ashram or climb the highest mountain to find the Divine – you just need to say to yourself, "I love me," "I am loved," "I am the Divine," "The Divine is me." You are all of these. Then intensely engage in feeling the Divine from within. It is the Divinity of all whereby one discovers serenity, and it is within the serenity of life where one finds the Divine. As you read the next chapters, you will be provided complete details on how to connect or reconnect to your Divine Essence. It is here within this feeling of connection or reconnection to the Divine, which is you, that you begin to realize that you are already an enlightened or *Light* perfect being.

As a meditation exercise, reconnect with this part of you; you may wish to simply move into a seated position facing an early-morning sunrise or evening sunset. Feel this peace-filled state of being. There are no words to describe this feeling – it is only a feeling, nothing more. Although, perhaps you could use the words *beautiful* and *pure space.* When you feel who you really are (the being within you), the Divine/Source/White Light, then know that everything is birthed from this place. It is this place of origin where everything will make itself known or reveal itself to you. Through these revelations, the spiritual evolution or transitioning will occur.

The first phase of this realization – that you are already enlightened – is being energetically released to all people between now and December 21, 2014. How it is being released is through various sources: people communicating with each other through books, spiritual leaders, courses, and more. This is the first phase within the new Mayan calendar. This phase is called the "preparation phase" and remains in effect from now until December 21, 2014. This is a preparation phase for people to awaken to the realization that they are already enlightened. They just need to feel, know, and live this and realize they are already where they need to be.

However, individuals begin to believe everything that they were told as children – even as early as the fetus stage. We should be aware that the fetus will feel and sense the mother's worry and anxieties. This communication of emotion in the fetus stage will send the message that *the world is a scary place,* and *I feel worried and anxious.* The fetus, when it is born, may already have acquired this impression or imprint upon his/her energy field and thoughts. This transferred programming begins to develop destructive and nondestructive thoughts, feelings, ideas, or opinions. As a child, one starts to believe this input from all adult sources. This is where and when the breakdown or breaking up of who you are truly starts.

When you begin to believe these false beliefs, you allow the ego to manage your life. The ego states that you are not good enough in all areas of your life – thus ignites the breakdown of your true authentic self. This breakdown is almost inevitable because you are a child of vulnerabilities and you have come to trust all adults. Now as an adult who feels and understands in a mature fashion, you become aware that everything and all things stem from the opinions and ideas of all your adult peers. However you are the Divine, the one who is enough, perfect, complete, whole, beautiful, confident, and still. Once awakened to this, you prepare for your new way of being.

This is the second phase of the original world, existing between 2015 and the end of 2018. This phase known as the "transition phase" is when areas in your life change and transform your way of living. These areas of transformation are fully described within the All Truths chapters of this book. For instance, in this transformational phase you may become more aware of your physical health, emotions, spiritual self, your relationships, and how you relate to your community. Reconnecting to nature will also be an important aspect. Also you will automatically move into a simpler, more grounded lifestyle.

Plus the gradual dismantling of different scientific theories and philosophies by scholars, such as Einstein and Abraham Maslow's hierarchy of basic human needs will become apparent (this new hierarchy is revealed within the pages of this book). We are entering into a gentler and simpler time of existence. Some individuals may resist the transformational shift. The majority will realize the shift as a potential for living a more joyful way of being.

The third and final phase (at least until it is time to reveal the other preceding phases) is called the "metamorphosis phase," which is similar to a butterfly emerging and recognizing it has wings and can take flight. This phase takes place from the beginning of 2019 and onward, when individuals are teaching, recognizing, and feeling the sense of freedom as living their original selves. It was once believed that the Mayan calendar ends on December 21, 2012. Many people have indicated through books, university studies and have learned much by crawling on the ground conducting digs, using a tiny, little brush dusting off minute Mayan symbols, while seeking the discovery of possible words or intellectual pieces of wisdom to explain the ending and the new beginning of the calendar.

The Mayans channeled system of formulating and messaging the prophecies of scribed language and symbols created their calendar through to the perceived date of December 21, 2012, at least this is what people believed. However, they actually did prophesize post-2012 without the use of symbols. What this means is defined as "the removal of all intellectual properties of discovery," meaning the removal of all symbols, words, scripts … everything!

So don't you see, dear reader, they did complete beyond 2012 by purposely not completing it. This explanation lies within their channeled form, which is described in further detail in this book. The Mayans already prophesized these time phases of "preparation, transition, and metamorphosis." The wait was intentional in order for the energy to shift and expose the one simple sign that denotes the new Mayan calendar which is revealed in this book. It is within this calendar where the Spirit of self exists and the *new beginnings* are exposed, the existence of Spirit/Divine encompassing love, peace, passion, compassion, and grace. It is within this context that one is able to *know, allow,* and *believe* the next stage or step of life as depicted in the new Mayan calendar. It really is pure and simple – nothing more.

I want you to keep in mind that as the Divinity of Love/White Light/Source is awakened or realized the ego awakens as well. With the ego come the fears, anxieties, worries, doubts, intellectual explanations, and more. It is the intention of ego for humans to live or vibrate at a very low level of fear and worry. Therefore when the topic of love surrounding soul's purpose, beauty of life in all beings, and more is discussed, then the ego or darkness steps in to put a stop to this. I recommend you don't pay any attention to ego as it just wants you to remain stuck in an illusion and not move forward in life. It wants you to remain behind in its lower vibration. You may experience thoughts, ideas, and energies that prevent you moving forward into your original self – just ignore these and continue moving forward. Release yourself into who you really are and then you will realize what is transpiring – nothing more than knowing you are the vibrant White Light!

In effect, life is spiritually wrapping itself more intensely around your choice of how you live in this world. You will learn how to exist in a most magnificent way that will *re-vibrate* the world.

The *re-vibration of the world* involves all people recognizing they are One with Spirit. Oneness is the key to existence and quite frankly that is all there is – Oneness! When awakened to who you truly are, a person of love, everything is connected with being, living, and existing in the moment. Communication is the key factor in the original world, which is constantly evolving. Communicating the following Spirit-filled information is most vital during these times.

As more and more people congregate in the newly formed way of being, the energy vibration of the planet rises. This energy is comprised of the vibration of goodness, love, peace, joy, and bliss. As a result, the ego begins to dismantle and loosen its hold. Suffering becomes lessened as more people become attuned to the truth of what is really happening in the world today. The truth is *realizing you are already enlightened* and nothing more than this! In its simplest form, you just need to engage in the following:

1. Being aware that you are already enlightened.
2. Being aware of living in the present moment.
3. Being aware of everything that is going on around you everywhere! In other words, when sitting or walking in a garden, are you aware of your feet landing upon the belly of Mother Earth? Are you aware of the magnificent songs springing forth from the softly colored birds? Are you aware of the butterfly flying around the purple flowers to your right? Are you aware of the big fat bumblebee

teasing you as it buzzes around your fingers just at
the moment you touch the red rose?

4. Be consciously aware that you are Spirit living in
   human form. You are Spirit/Source working through
   this vessel or instrument: the human form.

An original world is birthing itself! More children are being
born into this world who are very quickly understanding who
they really are and conveying comforting words like, "I need
to help the world." More adults are surrendering to this greater
land of Spirit and realizing there is more to life. Furthermore,
now that the Age of Aquarius or the original world reigns,
become engaged in living your life as you feel you should live it
in order to help it – meaning the Earth. Give the Earth a helping
hand. We need to raise the vibration of the planet in order to
continue onward and forward in a peace-filled manner.

This doesn't mean that the world will end if people don't
come to the realization of who they are. The more people who
realize they are Spirit in human form – meaning all beings are
Spirit – the better. This is truth and this is what the push about
2012 and post-2012 is all about. Therefore post-2012 is a line of
recognitions, a time of recognizing what is really transpiring. It
is a time also of preparing. One must prepare for the dawning
of the original world. When this time approaches, this dawning
of this age will occur. People need to prepare for this energetic
shift. And in fact, the preparation is already occurring. What
this means is that people are becoming more aware of ego, grace,
Spirit, soul's purpose, authentic self, living in the now, being
present, and being aware of what is going on around them.

As these terms and ideas, thoughts, and opinions spring forth, then more people will realize what is occurring on the planet is beauty, peace, passion, blessings, joy, and grace. And that when these spiritual emotions are felt and lived through humans in an authentic fashion, then this energy or Spirit resonates throughout the entire planet, thus creating a rejuvenation.

It is wise then to develop your way of being at this time and for you to do the following:

1. Grow up and out of your state of believing you are a victim.
2. Get over yourself and realize this isn't about you. It is about serving the planet!
3. Become awakened to who you really are – Spirit. Live deeply from this place of Spirit.
4. Live in the present moment because this is all there is right now!
5. Move into the awareness that you are already peace or a solidity of stillness. You are still.
6. Become fully engaged in being a surrendered self or recognizing that you are free!
7. Arrive in your place of self, that self which is held high through your authentic self. It is a place where you create that life you have been birthed to create. Live according to who you really are – a being of peace, an instrument of peace to serve. This is clearly pieced/peaced together in St. Francis of Assisi's poetic words, as below:

St. Francis of Assisi Prayer

Lord, make me an instrument of your peace.
Where there is hatred, let us sow love;
where there is injury, pardon;
where there is doubt, faith;
where there is despair, hope;
where there is darkness, light;
and where there is sadness, joy.
O Divine Master, grant that I may not so
much seek to be consoled as to console;
to be understood, as to understand;
to be love, as to love.
For it is in giving that we receive;
it is in pardoning that we are pardoned;
and it is in dying that we are born to eternal life
Amen

St. Francis of Assisi (1181–1226)

Embrace the New Way of Being – Freedom

This dawning of the New Age or the original world will be a time when all people are able to see, feel, hear, and taste the new way of living or being. What this means is that this new way of being is the deepest form of existing in the dawning of this age. This means that deep within the soul and Spirit of who you are is a truth, a deepness of reality – a solidity of joy, stillness, peace, passion, compassion, and freedom. It is now time to embrace this way of being.

It is a time when all people will be engaged in a choice that will inevitably take them to a new place of existing, a new place of realization, a new place of living. What is really occurring is the fact that all people are being placed in an arena of choice. You may or you may not choose to be in the choice of living a love-filled life or not. This is not to say that if you don't choose love you are doomed. All this simply means is that you have chosen and your life is thus wrapped around your choice – that is all! It only means that the intensity of the energies is more fluid or available in 2012 and post-2012 than ever before. It means that life is wrapping itself spiritually around each being more intensely and seeking your choice of how to live in this world – how to exist in a most magnificent way, a way that could in fact *re-vibrate the world.*

This re-vibration of the world entails simply this: all people recognizing they are One with Spirit and this Oneness is the key to their existence, and it is quite frankly nothing more than this. This is all it is! You see, when one is awakened you recognize who you truly are: a person of majestic qualities. It all ties in here with being, living, and existing in the moment – the now! Living here in present time means recognizing your nowness or your Spirit.

Once you realize who you are or you are awakened to who you are, then and only then does the original world begin for you. You see, it is not just the exterior of your world but also what pertains to your inner self.

It begins with one person recognizing his or her awakened state followed by another person and then another with a gentle rippling effect. One person at a time is realizing an awakening has occurred. From this rippling effect, more and more individuals are discovering this new way of being.

A vibration of energy is created by the new way of being, which swirls and whirls an incredible excitement around peace, joy, love, and grace. This new way of being is a new or higher vibration, which evolves into a most masterful way of existing. This heightened vibration from several people exudes an energy force that will facilitate an energetic shift for the entire planet. Much like the streaming of a golden thread from the Divine, that connects the entire universe.

If all people or at least the majority were to vibrate at this high energy level of being awakened, then the Earth, seas, sky, humans, all plants, and all animals would become filled with a beauty of freedom and releasing. Some would even say "a healing." This is not an indication that earth, sky, humans, all plants, and all animals are existing in a state of fear. This is simply stating that the illusion of the belief that all is fear needs to be *dismantled*. It is within this dismantling or releasing experience where freedom will reveal itself to you.

The first movement to embrace freedom is through you and only you. It is your choice. All humans have this free will choice. It is here and now this choice of freedom presents itself. Within or wrapped around this freedom are realization and awakening. This is the beginning of your new life or world. The new way of being has already entered into existence for you through reading these words stationed gratefully as messages within this book. Even if you do not read this book in its entirety, just by having it near you will be most *releasing* and *real-easing*. Just to carry it around or place it on a shelf will still bring goodness to your life because of its high vibration in energy.

The Oneness = The New Mayan Calendar = Spirit

ll of life is *One* with *Source* or whatever term you wish to call the *One Creator*. When you are engaged and involved within the Oneness of self, you begin to examine the truth and the possibility of being awakened to the realization that all of life is filled with just that – the Oneness. This Oneness is the completeness of yourself with the purity and the assuredness of love or Source. What this means is that all of nature – everything in nature including human beings – are together as Spirits connected to Source. This Oneness is the new post-2012 Mayan calendar, which appears simply like this:

The New Mayan Calendar Post-2012

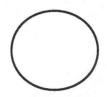

New Mayan Calendar Post-2012 (Figure 1)

Old Mayan Calendar 2012 (Figure 2)

- Nothing more and nothing less than just a silver circle. A line of silver energy in a circled form.
- Silver is depicting the gentleness, ease of Spirit.
- Silver contains the pure, clean, and clear energy. It is within the Oneness where all beings resonate.
- Silver is representing the energy of crystals.
- There are no symbols or illustrations within this New Post-2012 Mayan calendar. Unlike the old Mayan calendar which displayed many symbolic illustrations (see Figure 2).

The Mayans already realized the post-2012 calendar and knew that the next piece of their calendar or the prophesized calendar was a circle depicting Oneness. It is here within the Oneness where all people are able to discover serenity, peace, calmness, and stillness in all aspects of living. This Oneness purity of the life circle is stating that now is the time to restart life – to begin the *origin* of life, which is the completeness of the circle. What this means is the circle is never ending – always complete, always intact, always open and accepting. It greets itself to all beings and allows all beings to become part of it – that is all! It is the holding pattern of everybody and all of nature and therefore becomes the circle.

The New Mayan circle is the depiction of life after 2012. It is a time when all beings will slowly slide into the new way of existing or living called the Homo-Luminous way of existing. The Homo-Sapiens way of being is the human form that relates to the hunter/gatherer. The Homo-Luminous form of existing is one of pure Light and the realization that you are Light. This form is one of trust, passion, peace, love, and grace. This form will evolve fully by the year 3012 or perhaps before this time. It evolves around the beauty that *all* are the solidity of Spirit. Within this solidity of Spirit are the peace and the passion, which are filled with White Light or in other words the luminous body or Spirit body. This luminous body or Spirit form is beautifully illustrated in *Sacred Mirrors*, a 1990 book by Alex Grey. He illustrates how the White Light Spirit melds into the form thus creating the purity of Spirit only. His book is filled with illustrations supporting the spiritual transformation or evolution. It is a time for all people to recognize that life is just this, Spirit. A place of love.

When existing or living from this place of Spirit, everything is understood and completely felt. As you shift into all that life offers you, which is spiritually based, you then realize that all of life's pieces fit together miraculously. However, this is not a miracle but a way of being and believing.

The Mayans already knew about this world of origin or the original world. They spoke about its full history and spiritual evolution, evolution of the Spirit in human form. The evolution or movement into stillness, beauty, love, joy, and peace. Not of ego, fear, worry, and angst. This evolution to the original world has been metamorphosing for thousands of years. It is here within this state of existing that everything leads to the Oneness – the evolution to *One*. The planet is in a time of great evolutions, revolutions, and realizations – all leading up to living a fully awakened state.

The theme between 2012 and post-2014 is *Oneness*, which equals Spirit. Once awakened to this Oneness, you are then able to retrieve what you are seeking, which is a sense of belonging to the age of Oneness or origin because *Oneness* means "origin." Origin of life begins with the Spirit thus recognizing you are Oneness with Spirit. Therefore Oneness and origin are *One* in the same.

The first receivers of the pre-2012 Mayan calendar's information or the prophecies were the Mayans, Incas, and other ancient wisdom peoples. They proceeded to create within their script their symbols, music, drama, art, and dance. They were able to achieve all that was necessary in order to create the intellectual property of the prophecies. The original Mayan 2012 calendar contains several symbols that have been studied, examined detail by detail, researched, discussed, and conferenced (see Figure 2, page 28). However, the new Mayan calendar is devoid of all symbols (see Figure 1, page 28). It doesn't require a symbol. The circle is only used as script for the human in order to understand visually. The meaning and the symbol represents the Mother Earth, Father Sky, all of nature and human beings connecting as One with Spirit. The utter simplicity conveys this feeling.

Within this silver formed circle are crystal energies contained within a bed or catacombs of crystals. These catacombs live gently under the sacred places and spaces around the universe as energetically through Spirit. Examples of these places are the pyramids in Egypt and the Mayan ruins (Chichen Itza) in Mexico and Guatemala. Scribed within these crystal catacombs are the mystic laws or truths about the shift that is presently occurring. The term *scribed* means "one writes exactly what one hears or feels." In other words, Source/White Light is messaging and the Spirit or soul then scribes the messages energetically upon the Crystal Collectives, which in turn creates the All Truths or the mystic laws. These All Truths have been channeled from Edgar Cayce and Spirit through me to you. As stated earlier, Edgar Cayce was a mystic channeler who has kept these All Truths or prophecies within the Oneness circle. These All Truths are now being released and described in detail within this book.

You may wish to live these Truths or not. It's all about free will – you choose the way toward the White Light of self to grace or away from the White Light of self toward ego. This was the last part of the Mayan calendar: *free will* or the *will to choose freedom.*

This Is the Day – The *Now* Time for Exposure

For this is the day – the nowness of what is occurring on this planet. Here lie the energies and the spiritual connections to all beings. Within the temple of himself/herself, everything is created through the generous work of Source – don't you see how wonderful this adventure of living a most extraordinary life is? Don't you see how extraordinary life can be and is? It is engaged always with who you are. It is fully engaged with everything you do, hear, taste, touch, and think. Everything about your life resonates then from choice and nothing more than choice. The choice or free will remains within yourself as a spiritual inner being of love and peace or as a being who feels and believes in separateness from all beings.

Who are you and where do you come into play here? In other words, are you connected to Spirit of self, or are you connected to a part separate from you named ego? You see, ego will declare you as separate from Spirit. It sounds almost as if it – the ego – is a completely separate force or source from you – and yes it is. You may have declared it as a part of you. It may be that part that you have allowed into your belief system and therefore feel quite confident that your *ego* is who you are – nothing more! Edging God Out or Edging Grace Out! This is it and nothing more than this! So why not fess up and say the following to the ego? "Enough already. I have listened to you and believed you and maybe even identified myself through you, but now I caught you and now my life, my ideas, thoughts, feelings, all of myself is going to change and change for the better – nothing else matters – I am Spirit and no longer ego and never was ego."

Everything in life rides upon and lives from the fact that all beings are in essence, Spirit. How *on earth,* on the original Earth can ego survive when this time and post-2012 is based upon Spirit and not ego? More humans are becoming engaged in knowing, believing, and allowing their Spirit to reign. Therefore the ego will indeed disappear and at a very dramatic speed or fashion, so much so that many human beings will change their whole way of existing. They may switch their jobs, relationships, and more. If your identity is built upon ego, then you are allowing yourself to be driven away from your true self of Spirit. To be more specific, as you continue to move into the world of Spirit, White Light of love, authentic self, peace, and purpose on the planet, then the law of attraction or the law of Spirit will give you more of this experience of the White Light of Love. If you live from the experience of ego, then the experience and the way of being through ego will indeed be given to you. That is all! This is called the law of attraction or the law of Spirit. Begin to examine your way of being and detect and listen very carefully how you live your life – through Spirit/Grace or Ego.

Here is the key point: within 2012 and post-2012 life as all humans know it will be different. As you can see, a lot of literature, conferences, TV shows, films, and more are speaking about ego and the Spirit of White Light. The awareness is definitely emerging. This awareness is part and parcel about the movement and preparation from now until December 21, 2014, the transforming beginning 2015 until the end of 2018, and then the metamorphosing from 2019 onward. This is not news to Spirit and for many humans. It is time for the ego to be dismantled. This is a very important statement because when living within the age and the following year ages of 2012 and still believing the ego, then you will not fully appreciate the shift that is occurring on the planet and you may in fact slide more deeply into the ego's illusion – this is the problem. However, you do have *free will*, which means the *will to be freed* from ego or remain in a separateness by living through the ego.

The original world exists within the hearts of all people. So why not awaken to who you really are. Within truth there is freedom, liberation, authenticity, love, peace, trust, and stillness. It is here within the awakened state where the reasons of the truth and the decisions for the truth are made. When in an awakened state, everything changes. For example, when reading this book you will begin to see, feel, hear, taste, and touch life differently from the spiritual perspective. This original world is not just within the hearts of people but within the hearts of Mother Earth, Father Sky, the universe, planets, and all plants and animals. It is here within the energy Source where all beings live from and through.

Spirit knows exactly what is going on during these times. However, human beings need to live this original world or new existence, which really is an old existence, from within themselves, otherwise they may live an ego-based life. But let's examine this further. Be aware that people can become so introspective and believing that they are so awakened they may become isolated and then separate from others – this is also the emergence of ego once again. Even some spiritual leaders or teachers begin to believe and feel that they are true prophets and require absolute extra special treatments, large sums of money, and more. This is ego! As explored further revealing the Essence of 2012 and post-2012 moving into 2013, remember that these times of great change and *new beginnings* is about being awakened to Spirit and then living from this place. This is interior moving through an exterior form of being.

When reflecting back on history, you will notice several hundreds of years of ego-driven civilizations, which include war, greed, selfishness, cleansing of race, and slavery. Now, yes, of course this is still occurring even at a subtle level of existence. However, when one becomes awakened, one then begins to see the action of the ego through the human and you can then say something, send White Light, change something, choose an action or topic to help remove poverty, war, and abuse on children.

See how this works now? Being awakened means being alert, alive, no longer sleeping within the bed of the ego but rising up into the Spirit of aliveness. These are exciting times for all beings because of the shifting that will occur over these next few years. In fact, this shifting is already happening.

What is starting to occur within these times is the disappearance of intellectual ideas, thoughts, reasons, and beliefs, and the Spirit is now in the driver's seat. In other words, people are now feeling and flowing first and then allowing the intellect to come forth. Allow the Spirit and the emotion to flow and then allow the thinker intellect to assist in the flow of Spirit. When you allow this sequence of emotion, then intellect and life can transition with ease and in some cases quickly and surely. Therefore, if the driver's seat is the intellect or thinker and the assistant is the Spirit or emotion, then this tends to not be effective and it is affecting who you are – your authentic self. One cannot think the Spirit into something. You see what this means? It's like this, for example: you get on a bus and tell the driver exactly where you need to go and what time to leave and how long the trip should be and which seat will be yours instead of arriving on the bus and allowing the driver to take you where you should go in order to live the process. You know that the driver is the emotion and Spirit and you feel the driver knows where to go and all you do is show up. All you know is that the driver is going in the absolute perfect place, direction, on time, has the perfect seat for you, and is never late or lost. This example explains that the driver of your life is always the flow of Spirit and the thinker/intellect is the follower – never the other way around. The original world or the new beginning will be a time when people dissolve the driver-seated thinker or intellect. It is a time when the empowerment and/or the power of Spirit reigns and the intellect/thinker assists. Imagine the beauty of this new world. This type of world then has many different aspects to it than the world that exists now. This new world includes:

1. Egoless
2. Self led only by the flow of Spirit
3. The thinker intellect as assistant to Spirit

Abraham Maslow and some other greats, if living during these times, would speak more about their spiritual connection to the Divine and subsequently create new inventions, ideas, thoughts, music, and art. In fact, as indicated, this original world is actually old Earth, old newness, and an old original way of being. It is being implemented or created – symbolically as a circle. In other words it is the beginning of time again. Time to recreate and co-create with everyone, including Mother Earth, Father Sky, fish, animals, plants, and so on. Everything is being recreated, reshuffled, or reorganized in order for the world to fulfill its soul's purpose. Its purpose is to emulate love, peace, and joy. In order for its fulfillment to occur, the Spirit of the awakened self of being needs to blossom forth. It is a time when the White Light of love shines forth brightly and create Oneness within the belly of Mother Earth and the arms of the Father Sky.

In the beginning (if one believes in time) all was created, all was organic and original. However, even when in this organic state of existence (indigenous peoples/natives) there existed ego, war, greed, abuse, and so how is this different from today? Not so much. Humans today just have more of sophistication in their ego.

But what needs to be pointed out here is the following: the origin of time of creation through Spirit has always been just that – origin. Realize that time is an illusion, it is used to place information in a contextual way. The illusion of time will immediately be revealed during the years of the original world, in other words the years of preparation (until end of 2014), transition (2015 to the end of 2018), and metamorphosis (post-2019). The origin when this is recognized through Spirit is the beauty within love, peace, and stillness. This point of origin of Spirit was miraculous and filled with wonder and amazement and all was clear. This *clarity* is called the origin – nothing more than this but origin.

When you retreat back to your origin (your initial state of being) you discover that Spirit and only Spirit is the origin (for lack of a better word). You then move or *shift* into that part of you that is awakened by you – the human form. Don't worry. This Spirit is always alive and giving you signs and hints that you are Spirit – it is just waiting for you to awaken to it and for you to recognize it, thus awakening to the origin of you! So this term called "original world" is actually the perfect term to use. The Earth is returning to its origin – the origin of the planet is now returning! This is the shift and the new Mayan calendar.

Returning to the One who is you – as sung in mantra by Jennifer Berezan on her CD *Returning* (Berezan, Jennifer. *Returning.* Edge of Wonder Records. 2000). Returning to the origin of who you are – Spirit. Everything on this planet of origin or this planet of returning will stream from Spirit. This is the only way it (being life) will be able to function properly and effectively through Spirit. This is the only way!

All theories, philosophies, ideas, ideals, thoughts, opinions, mathematical equations, and spiritual theories, will all be reshaped and redesigned to suit this new way of living. It is here within these redesigns where the Spirit or the flow of Spirit is the designer with the assistance from the thinker intellect of self without ego. It is during this time in place or this moment or millisecond of now where all creation will be recreated.

In other words, as people live in the moment of now – the existence or the presence of being present – then the flow of Spirit has more access and fluidity through the form named *human body.* All decisions will be made only from this place of Spirit, stillness, and love, and in fact this will eliminate war, greed, abuse, sabotage, and selfishness.

The Crystal Palace

The All Truths are scribed energetically within the catacombs of the Crystal Palace, which is the energy structure holding and binding the ancient sacred places, such as Chichen Itza, Tikal, the Pyramids, and others. The Crystal Palace is the energy that all sacred places were built from and upon. This Crystal Palace of energy systems holds the information energetically and spiritually and is now making itself known, realized, and exposed. What is occurring is that the Pyramids, ancient Mayan writings, Tikal, Chichen Itza, Mayan calendar, and the Inca symbols are dissolving and what is being exposed is the following: a beautiful grace-filled Crystal Palace that will reveal all that is necessary for not only the *preparation time* from now until the end of 2014 but also the *transition time* from 2015, the end of 2018, and then the *metamorphosis* of 2019 and beyond, some further steps which have not been fully revealed as yet!

This Palace is a large catacomb of white-clear crystals of all sizes clumped together and called Collectives. At the bottom of the front cover of this book illustrates what these collections of crystals may look like within the Crystal Palace. These collections of crystals deal specifically with certain spiritual areas in an energetic fashion. For example, one Crystal Collective contains the All Truth (mystic laws) messages scribed upon the energetic scrolls whose message contains new philosophies. Another collective contains the scribed work of Oneness, and so on. Not only were the All Truths scribed on the energy scroll but so is everything else that needs to be now released and exposed.

All of the Truths are saying, "Now is the time." The present time is now – a time of great exposure will occur and is occurring in the purity of love ... This love is so pure that only small portions at a time will be exposed. Exposure of all of this information will occur within its perfect timing. Therefore, the amount of information channeled for you through this book is just the right amount for now!

It is within this perfect timing where the exposure occurs, but it is also within the readiness of the planet, humans, Father Sky, Mother Earth, and all beings. For example, if an intense push concerning dismantling the ego occurred hundreds of years ago, then it may have been considered as mundane, crazy, worthless; but slowly this form of discussion has been building up until this moment in history and now is the time, no doubt about it! All is perfect!

Now is the time for all people to begin to realize that the most important part of all of this is simply their own awakening because the Crystal Palace and all of its grace is exposing itself as the intellectualized pieces decrease and disintegrate. It is through this disintegration of the intellectualization of the Earth whereby the Crystal Palace becomes fully exposed. It is not birthing itself but just simply exposing itself. It has always been around in an energy subtle fashion (which means it has already birthed) but now is opening its gates.

The Crystal Palace is one of delicate nature
and fine in its energy vibrations.
It is one of pure, crystal clear Spirit.

It is one of Divine nature and one of
solidity of stillness and peace.
It is one of greatness in self.
It is one that is fully connected with Spirit.
It is pure love at its highest form and vibration.
It is bright and glistening in nature.
It is strong in diamond quality – never
ending in energy and Spirit.
The Crystal Palace is the container for the
highest, finest vibration of information.
It is the container for the entire scroll of not only
the All Truths but the attainment of the highest
vibrational contextual energy patterns.

In other words, what this means is that the information that will be shared within these pages is from the Highest Christ Consciousness. The scrolls that have been energetically scribed are spiritual in nature. This place named the Crystal Palace is a place where all information has been stored and kept as sacred in this sacred place, and it is nothing more than this.

Therefore, in review, the beds or catacombs within the Crystal Palace are composed of the Crystal Collectives. The Collectives resonate at a very high frequency or vibration, which means the messages within the mystic laws or All Truths match the God/Source vibration. Each group of Crystal Collectives has several crystals and within each crystal is a message. These messages are scribed in a crystallized scroll through Spirit. Some of these scrolls with the scribed messages are now being opened and shared here within these pages. As mentioned, these messages were once considered mystic laws and are now being called the All Truths because the mystic laws indicate mystery and secrets only for a few. The All Truths are truths for *all* people. Therefore all people have access now to these All Truths. This is what this channeled book contains.

Remember the *original self* of all beings is evolving back to Spirit. In other words, the original self is Spirit evolving back to this original place. Some are calling this original self the Homo-Luminous form or the illuminated formless as compared to Homo-Sapiens. Simply put, the true self of Spirit is returning. When resonating from this original self, you are complete love, joy, peace, passion, and bliss. You see, feel, touch, taste, and hear all of what life offers differently and Divinely. You then realize that all are One. The Oneness is that all beings are Spirit and therefore all are connected to Source, to the Oneness. As the spiritual evolution described above shifts, moves, and circulates, the vibration of the planet rises and therefore creates a healing and rejuvenation throughout the world. This is called the Age of Aquarius.

These times are most exciting for all people. Now is the time to read and explore these scribed messages or All Truths as they are called within the crystallized scrolls as imprinted within each group of Crystal Collectives.

It is a time now for people to feel and know these All Truths and begin to reshape their lives into a more meaningful and awakened state. The revealing of these All Truths is occurring now because it is the time of the revelations or in other words a shift back to the original world or original self. As people transition into being awakened, they will become aware of these truths. So what does *awakened* mean again? It means to simply know, allow, and believe that you are Spirit first and human form second. You are a Spirit experiencing a human life. You have purpose, plan, and a spiritual journey as a human.

You are the vessel for the Spirit to move through you. You are the instrument that music is created by the Spirit. When you awaken to this realization, you then begin to feel and sense life very differently. You awaken to these All Truths of self, others, and the planet.

The term *awaken* is scribed heavily through the All Truths within the Crystal Collectives. When awakened, all of these All Truths become very clear – in fact, daily or even hourly or every second of your life, more and more awakenings will happen for you. These All Truths will just happen naturally. You will live and resonate at a higher vibrational level, which means that you will see, feel, touch, hear, and taste everything differently. In fact, when you resonate within a different vibrational level, you live a lightness of being and begin to acknowledge what is really going on. You begin to walk around the world feeling very light and warm. This feeling is one of stillness, assuredness, and trust. It is a feeling throughout the entire morning, afternoon, and evening of *being taken care of,* and really nothing more than this. So arise to this awakening and you shall see what happens – it will be beauty in its grandest of form.

Spirit is guiding the journey of these All Truths as people and the planet shift or evolve back to the original world and the original self. This is a spiritual promise.

All Truths

As stated in the last section, the All Truths are exposed through the Crystal Collectives. The All Truths are scribed upon the crystallized scrolls imprinted within the Crystal Collectives. These All Truths are the seeds for the original world and are intertwined within the shift of consciousness of people during these times of 2012 and post-2012.

As the original world sprouts, it requires healthy seeds, which are the All Truths; good soil, meaning people coming together to create a rich environment of Oneness; rain, which is the cleansing and *releasing into real-easing;* and finally the warmth of the sun, thus the high vibration of Spirit. And of course central to the All Truths is the Mayan calendar.

In review, the Mayan calendar post-2012 is a silver circle and within the central space of the circle are the crystal catacombs that contain the All Truths. Remember too that the crystal catacombs or beds are the basis or core of the Crystal Palace. And the Crystal Palace(s) is (are) energetically under the *sacred places* within the universe, which are held tightly through and by Spirit. Spirit therefore is guiding the journey of these All Truths as well as a cleansing.

Remember too this shift and the All Truths or the prophecies are gradual changes. These All Truth examples as stated below will not completely or fully occur before December 21, 2012. The examples are a small sampling of All Truths, and so many more that will be described as channeled in detail throughout this book.

1. New archangels are being formed to assist in the shift.
2. Ego diminishes and eventually completely dissolves because people are recognizing it as an illusion.
3. Dietary needs will change for all people.
4. The way of living will become different in a beautiful way of meaning.
5. Transportation changes will be more attuned to Mother Earth and Father Sky.
6. More people wanting to connect to nature through hiking, camping, gardens, and growing their own food.
7. Disease will diminish as people realize and are awakened to the emotional cause of dis-ease.
8. Knowledge and information sharing will also shift into nothingness.
9. Organic foods become more readily available.
10. Energies and the electrical patterns of electricity will also turn around in a most miraculous way.
11. The shift is within each person and outside each person. Each influences the other.
12. More courses will be facilitated concerning Oneness, being awakened, an authentic self, and so much more.
13. How Spirit approaches people and how energy is used and understood will also change.
14. Rhythm and music transition into higher vibrational music and lyrics.
15. Poets, writers, and artists will be connecting to Spirit more readily and with ease.
16. Education changes to match the shift:

a) Class sizes;

b) Style of teaching children.

17. Exercise patterns, eating habits, meditation, yoga, and spiritual practice all become focused, intensely discussed, and implemented.

18. The sun, moon, stars, and earth, as well as the north, south, east, and west, begin to change directions as the original Earth slowly shifts.

19. The water table slowly lowers in some areas dramatically and increases dramatically in other areas.

20. The axis of the earth tenderly moves.

21. The process of elimination occurs. Eliminating all that is unnecessary in one's life moves one forward into the process of illumination – a status of complete Oneness with Spirit.

22. The tides and the waves of the oceans transition in a most beautiful way. You shall see!

23. The winds that have been declared as westerly will no longer be westerly, but a whole new wind pattern will emerge.

24. The Spirit or energy body of each human being will evolve or reveal itself in an illuminated or Homo-Luminous fashion – meaning purity of soul, Spirit, and energy – rather than a Homo-Sapiens form.

25. The veil between the human solid form and Spirit form is thinning at a dramatic rate. Why? Because the *proof is in the pudding.* When people begin to see, feel, hear, and touch Spirits of others and beyond, the term *Spirit* becomes more accessible for many because you see more and more people are becoming attuned to the Spirit. People are speaking

about channeling, Reiki, mediumship, and being psychic.

26. Changes of cloud formations will occur as the patterns of weather also realign.

27. Heavy rain's and rapid winds arise in order to cleanse the earth – this is a clearing and communication from nature to humans saying, "Time has come. Awaken."

28. The old id, ego, superego, unconscious, and sub-conscious diminish to reveal the higher vibration of Oneness.

29. The energy of money redefines itself. Money becomes meaningless.

30. Companies, agencies, countries, and governments will become more aware of ego and grace.

31. The ways to honor Spirit, such as religious practices, will slowly disappear or develop into a newness of belief or knowing. Churches as you then know them now will diminish.

32. Technologies will become reorganized as realizations that there is *more to life than the sum total of technology/ computers.*

33. Reasons to serve and reasons to receive will be discussed, felt, and further implemented.

34. The idea that the God figure as only outside oneself will diminish and people will realize and believe that God or White Light is within and outside – it is all around. In fact you are God.

35. Spirit is remolding the Earth/universe with its hands upon the flexible clay of the world.

36. Due to the crisis of the environment at this present time, the salt in the oceans is restructuring in order to adapt to the environmental shifts and the toxicities.

37. The elements of water, wind, fire, earth, and ether will transition and change as according to the universal energetic shift.

38. More ascended masters are revealing themselves through spiritual connections.

39. Language is changing to a higher frequency. Certain words, such as *hate, war,* and *self-worthlessness,* will no longer exist.

40. Books and information of higher frequency reflecting Oneness, being awakened, and living your authentic self will be published.

41. Spirit – like people getting together rapidly and connecting to the shift of the new consciousness.

42. Discussions about: being in the now or present moment, living out of time, now has no time, time is irrelevant, and more will occur.

43. Movement toward an authentic way of being is accelerating at an enormous rate.

44. Recognition of poverty, homelessness, and other social inequalities will be examined and eliminated.

45. The way in which one moves into a therapeutic practice also is transitioning. The releasing of memories from trauma will occur faster and new information is gathered more quickly.

46. All beings on this planet will evolve and be created into a new being that will revolve around their

true Essence of self which is the Oneness ... more All Truths or prophecies are explored in detail throughout The All Truths section of this book.

Within all of these All Truths are the inner cavities of just pure nothingness. It is within this central core of this nothingness where the original world is being depicted as just a round circle. This circle is empty and filled with Spirit – with the void. The void or nothingness is the purity of Spirit – there is nothing within it and never will be. It is that which is within you. Within this void are the All Truths as scribed within the scrolls of the Crystal Collectives. These are not only energetically imprinted outside yourself but within your Essence, or your Spirit, as well! Within the purity of your Essence. It is the absolute core of this Oneness or the central component of the All Truths. This inner and most central core exists within each and every person including nature and has a vibration that can never be measured or recorded. It is within the inner beauty of the inside core of a flower in full bloom. It is the inside beauty of the long-legged deer that prances and dances from one woodland to another; it is that feeling you get right at the moment of viewing creation at its best. This could also be a newborn baby, a sunset, or the first moments a sprout pokes out of the belly of its Mother Earth. It could even be your first bite into a fresh wild berry. These feelings are all the same. This feeling is that core, is that central part of self, the indescribable self!

This core of self is the Source – the Creator, the central part of the All Truths. You feel this every minute when awakened because when you feel this feeling you then need to realize that this feeling is within you. You are this feeling! Your core is Source/Spirit – this feeling.

Visualize back to how you feel when gazing at that most spectacular sunset or sunrise and pull that feeling within yourself and then attach this feeling to you. This is love, peace, joy, and stillness. This is the being of completeness. You are this named Spirit. Next time you are viewing the beauty of a sunrise or sunset, remember that this beauty may be so overwhelming you can't even describe it.

This indescribable Oneness or feeling is that part of you that wants to be awakened. When living from this point of recognition of this feeling, all recognized points of living will be awakened and realized, and therefore you become spiritually evolved into this new form named Homo-Luminous. Homo-Sapiens means the human man and woman. But Homo-Luminous means Oneness with Spirit.

Therefore the core of the Homo-Luminous being is the core of All Truths. It is a feeling that is indescribable.

Because of the connection to this feeling, many people will wish, yearn, and long to connect to nature. What will occur, according to the All Truths, is that once you become awakened to who you are, which is this feeling, you then need nature around you because this feeling can be found in nature. Would you, for example, have this feeling while viewing and touching the next iPod invention? No, of course not, because it is not a being of Source from direct creation like that of a newborn fawn or a new peapod sprouting upon its mother's vine.

Back to nature in this the original world will be the main and most important theme in the next number of years. The connection or reconnection to nature is absolutely vital in order to rejuvenate this feeling. You will see many humans needing to go hiking up mountains, walking in a garden, planting, volunteering on a natural conservancy, leading groups to speak about nature, becoming activists for Mother Earth and Father Sky. As all of the Crystal Collective All Truths state, "Connecting back to your origin is now evolving into a need—a need to connect and feel this connection." Nature then becomes extremely important. In fact, some humans would say that their spiritual practice is always within nature. Nature is the driving force and place for beings to go to feel their connection.

Nature is also a place of great cleansing, clearing, and rejuvenating. As each person becomes awakened and realized, he or she then influences Mother Earth and Father Sky. This then increases the vibration of the Mother Earth and the Father Sky. This vibration then resonates within the planet, on the soil, in the trees, plants, sun, moon, stars, atmosphere, everywhere, and because of this, when you are walking in the forest, garden, hiking the mountain, and gardening, you will feel this high vibration and an immediate *feeling* connection occurs. A common, Source-filled, peace-filled, still feeling occurs, which is really stemming from *you*. You are that vibration, and when you connect with it through nature you are connecting back to you. There is much cleansing, clearing, and rejuvenating within nature.

It is through this feeling or this connection where artists, musicians, writers, poets, and all those who create, which is really everybody, connect into this Source of feeling to design or create what is to be created or birthed through them. Some creators or artists already know what they need to birth. They already know, feel, taste, touch, and smell exactly what they need to do.

This need is felt by all people, not just artists. Some authors know exactly what they need to write or birth. People who live a life in accounting, law, transportation drivers, hands-on workers, all *know* they have something to birth. This may be a new idea that came to them from *nowhere,* which really is a place – that void, emptiness, that stillness – that feeling. You see, the Source really works in amazing ways – some would say mysterious – but let's say, as the All Truths say, "all ways." This feeling of needing to birth something is the absolute core of who you are. Stemming from this feeling or this knowing is something that you need to wisely pay attention to. For this birth may be the next step along your golden path—your path of serving and receiving!

Pay attention to yourself and ideas, thoughts, feelings, and more as you read and reread and deeply feel all these All Truths. Each word on every page has been carefully and tenderly placed in a specific energetic order just for you. In the quiet spaces or breath gaps between the words are messages situated in absolute perfect order. Absorb gently.

Part II

The All Truths

The message of truth is based upon the inner dialogue between Source and the human, thus the *dimension of reality.*

Breathe

This Crystal Collective is messaging to you from its All Truth the fact that "all is in perfection and by breathing you will see, feel, hear, taste, touch, and smell that all is perfect." This perfection of Spirit is of course nothing more than this. When breathing in your human form or body, you are breathing all that needs to be breathed in order to live in this form called *body*. When breathing deeply, you are then moving your body into a place of stillness, peace, and silence, even if in a large bustling city or in the midst of a conflicting situation. Breathing breath through your form – your body – is absolutely vital. The breath is actually breathing you.

The breath is Source and it is breathing you – you aren't breathing it. When you reciprocate through the core of who you are, you are then breathing Spirit and Spirit is breathing through you! You are being breathed and you are breathing – both working together, Spirit and form in reciprocation. Both breathing each other and nothing more nothing less. When you are breathing deeply into your whole self, you are then entering more of an awareness, more of an entry into peace. Be aware of your every breath. Source can easily work through forms that are deeply breathing. How often do you hear a yoga instructor say, "Begin with your breath"? This is how you, a form, began – you began with breath. You were at this still point and breathed the breath of life, and now you decide to become awakened and reciprocate within the core of your relationship with Spirit.

When coming back to breath, you then shift into a peace-filled place and within this stillness you then find, hear, and feel intuition. Then your attunement comes into play, which means being attuned to self is actually being attuned to your breath first followed by the peace and stillness within this breath.

When you are engaged within your breath, you will notice that actually more oxygen will be given to you – the universe says, "I will give you more of this because you are asking for it." And in fact, when walking through a forest in deep breath and stillness, you will notice that you will begin to breathe more deeply and become still and peace-filled because, don't forget, you are One with nature. Nature will provide oxygen back to you immediately because it is reflecting or mirroring back to you what you are giving it: life, peace, bliss, stillness, and grace.

Look at all of these emotions connected to breathe and to add to it is love – love of self, love of life, love of all that is of life. When this is felt by you, you then give this out to the world and then the world will reflect and give this back to you! All are One! All are within breath. Within this breath, you will acquire a deeply creative self. This is the place whereby all artists connect with a creative idea, thought, song, dance, drama, and poem. This place of breath is where one finds intuition, guidance, Spirit, Oneness with all – this is it and all it starts with is breath. Breathe into you and you will be breathed. Then fill up with all of the most beautiful oxygen that will be given to and for you!

Recognize that:

Peace
Stillness
Love
and
Breath
Are
You!

Inner Authentic Self = Bliss!

This particular scribed message from the All Truths states the following: "Follow your bliss of who you are. This is the real you – the you that is created through and by Source. Source wishes for you to be just who you are, which is authentically encased and enveloping bliss!" Bliss is the only term to describe this in human language because there is no language to really describe this within the human.

Bliss really means "origin," which is Source and your sacred place. Connecting to your sacred place releases you into a formed bliss. The bliss is the feeling shining forth from the White Light of origin. When in bliss, you will truly know this – it is so obvious to others and to yourself that there may be times that you need to just rest and reconfigure your life.

Bliss can be almost overwhelming (in a good way!). Sometimes when humans first experience bliss, they may feel like they can't possibly move. This is extremely common. It is here within the bliss that miracles are formed. It is here within the bliss when people change their lives. Allow the bliss to settle first then move into decisions. When this *bliss* becomes integrated within you, you shift, which means your authentic self begins to shine through. Worries and anxieties drip away and melt like creamy hot chocolate, and the bliss then interprets your passion in life or your soul's purpose.

Your soul's purpose is your passion, which stems from your bliss. What then creates the most intense feeling of bliss in your life? Is it art, writing, music, volunteering, assisting children, environment, helping others awaken to their bliss, etc.? What is the passion for you? Perhaps a simple passion of just feeling free. Perhaps your soul's purpose is to just feel free in this life time. Remember too that tightly woven within bliss are love, stillness, and Essence. All three of these are who you are and you just need to realize this truth.

Furthermore, bliss in passion can take on a variety of forms. Bliss felt in human form has a much lower vibration than the Source – the full Source/God is bliss! In other words, the God/ Source cannot be fully felt because of the power of its vibration – and if felt would be too intense for a human being. You, as the human being, are able to feel part of the bliss. This bliss is one of a greatness that all humans have access to and are able to connect with through their decision of choosing the White Light.

The most important part in all of this information is choice. Choosing how you wish to lead your life is absolutely essential. It is through the choosing whereby life will change. You see, the reason this is being spoken about within this book of 2012 and post-2012 is because the time of living through Spirit/ authentic self or bliss has arrived. The original world will be based souly/solely upon *and only upon* the Source's White Light as it manifests itself through bliss. Scribed upon the scrolls of life within the Crystal Collective is "living through Spirit" and feeling this bliss, feeling the integration of this bliss and arriving at this place.

See how very easy this is and how this decision can be made in an instant. This feeling of bliss can be felt in an instant. It begins with your decision and simply your decision – this is why the choice or decision is extremely important. This is the key decision!

To review this All Truth, keep in mind that the crystal scrolls entail all that is relevant for today – this day! This particular Crystal Collective dealt with your inner self or inner wisdom. It is who you are – the bliss, the inner self, the wise self, the One. This is probably the most important Crystal Collectives to start with. It also involves creating the authentic life that is filled with passion and authentic ways of being.

Examine How You Live

Begin to examine how you live, where you live, what you eat, what you wear, and so on because the shift is about rejuvenating your life in such a way that you are paying close attention to your lifestyle. The Crystal Collectives' All Truths are indicating that "One should re-examine how one lives. Do you eat organic foods? Are you supporting Mother Earth and Father Sky? Are you perhaps growing your own food? Are you creating a lifestyle that is positive and in high vibration? Are you creating a job that matches who you are and what you believe?" All of these and more questions need to be further explored and examined during 2012 and post-2012. These questions will be of utmost importance.

As the original world begins to reveal itself, so too does the *original way* of existing – this way was living off the land and creating a simple, yet serving and receiving way of existing. Some people have always lived this way. Keep in mind as well that many people live in larger cities with their jobs, families, houses, and friends. How on earth, they may ask, are they going to be able to live this ideal lifestyle? Remember for some people this is symbolic and representational. For example, if you live in a city of a million people, you still create community. You will and can create a simple and easy lifestyle, and in fact the larger city allows you to connect with others who share the same ideas, theories, feelings, awareness, etc. Perhaps you have a small garden or perhaps you purchase organic foods from the local shop and wear recycled clothing. No matter where you live, you can still create a simple way of being. This is why the term *simplicity* has been coming forward for many years, because it is now time to take simplicity seriously. The All Truths state this very clearly!

Knowing

This All Truth message is one that wraps itself around the *one thing* or *the key*, which is the core message from all of the Crystal Collectives: "the knowing." The feeling of all! In other words, when you live a sense of knowing, which means a deep internal sense of peace or stillness, you live from the place of origin, great peace, and tranquility, that place of completeness, all of which is Spirit, your original self. When you discover this place, you then discover a peace. The knowing is Spirit. It is the place where everything resonates from and it is here within this part of self you discover that this is who you really are. You are that knowing. You are that part of self, which is of love, peace, joy, and bliss.

When you begin to become your knowing, you begin to see and feel differently because what happens is that all pain and suffering just melt away and you then immediately release all that you don't require. You release into the knowing of who you really are. You begin to see and feel as if you have finally arrived to whom you are, which is thus called *the knowing*.

It is here within the knowing where all knowledge, wisdom, and information are understood then dismantled. Knowledge, wisdom, and information will no longer exist because the knowing or the Spirit of self overrides these mindful/ intellectual terms. It is here within this knowing that everything becomes alive in wonder, love, and peace because the knowing is just that – a deep knowing, a feeling, and not an intellectual capability but an innate quality of just being in Spirit. It is here within this knowing and being in Spirit where you become filled with who you are. The knowing is already within you. It is already you! And nothing more. What does this translate into? You are God/Source/White Light. This is who you really are. There is not intellectual knowledge within the God/Source/White Light because life is just being. Life is just an *isness*. Life is joy.

You take the word *knowledge* and dismantle it down to *knowing how to live on the edge*, knowing how to exist in this world and living from this deep inner place of just knowing. This place is a deep peace-filled feeling, a place you can live and exist in completeness. It is a place you can maintain and contain your way of being, which is within the knowing and nothing more than this. Therefore wisdom and the knowledge are already intertwined within your knowing. That is all! That is it!

Promise and Hope Are Within

This Collective is a grand one in "promise and hope." What this means is that if you feel and believe that there is no hope or promise from Source, then you are very sadly mistaken. This All Truth states "all of the promises and hopes are within you and you just need to tap into its Source or Spirit. It is you!"

The promises and the hopes are within you and only within you. You will not find your promises and hopes in anybody else. This is truth. The truth you seek is already within you and nowhere else but within you. You are the truth, nothing more than this! These promises are made by Source. Also note that where these promises and hopes reside, you will also discover happiness followed by bliss, which is comfort, peace, grace, passion, and compassion. Within each of these are the qualities of who you really are – nothing more than this! Become engaged in your inner being, your inner self, the true being of who you really are. One of promise and hope. It is within this stance where you discover more of who you are.

In fact, as the awakening continues, you will notice that even your laughter will change and your face will soften. Many pieces and parts of yourself will shift and change. You will notice more and more of this as you shift your life.

A being of White beautiful Light – you are nothing more than this! A White Light being of hope and promise. Once you realize this, you are then obligated to assist others who are also seeking promise and hope. Within the promise and the hope are the bliss, peace, comfort, grace, passion, and compassion. It is within these feelings whereby all things occur. When you discover this most incredible truth that is just within you, you then settle into your awakened state. You then have arrived and have awakened to this great state of being.

What is also being stated by the All Truth is that, as one becomes attuned to who one really is, then one arises to a situation of being reorganized, rearranged, and reshifted into the *highest self of being.* This means that when you arise to being awakened, you then become engaged in the creation, recreation, and co-creation of your life.

Become aware of all that is for you. Accept the gifts to you in order for you to transform your entire life or metamorphosis into a grand being that you already are. You just need to become awakened to this and all the promises and hopes will flood to you as this gift. You will discover that several gifts come your way as you open up, allow, receive, give, believe, and know that abundance is arriving and is actually already here.

Living

A ccording to these next clusters or Collectives of Crystals, what one needs to achieve is full recognition and realignment to self. All plants, animals, people, water, air, and all beings are equal, and according to the All Truths "all are One therefore equal." There is no inequality anymore. For centuries upon centuries, inequality existed and still may exist and be the truth for many humans. However, the truth and the deepest core of truth state that "all are One." If you hurt another, you hurt yourself and those whom you love. Yes, this does include plants, animals, the sea, Father Sky, rocks, minerals, and all living beings. The stream of the "consciousness of One" is just that! A *stream* that moves through all beings and in a flowing most beautiful manner. This is truth and everyone in Spirit or inspired knows this. This is the only way to exist in life, through the Oneness of and about Spirit, nothing more than this! All beings have been delivered upon this planet for reasons, and that one core reason is to love. Love oneself first and then this love will emulate toward others. This is called *living*.

Become engaged with the Oneness of yourself and realize that you are just that, One! One being – one self! One person, but only a one within the Oneness of all. For example, you become the fullness of self with the Oneness once you discover that you are one with yourself—one of self and One with all people.

You then begin to feel not alone anymore but together with all people and beings. You begin to allow a sense of completion reside through and around you in a most beautiful way. You then know and allow the Oneness to occupy you!

For many people, loneliness, depression, anger, frustrations, and so on all disappear in an instant. Kaboom! In a snap, gone! Over! What occurs is an awakening to another realization or a realization to further awakenings. These realizations will occur frequently once awakened.

When you realize that you are already an enlightened being, you then realize that new revelations are being revealed and are actually the revitalizations of the planet. In other words, the All Truths are the new revelations or rather old revelations that are simply revitalizing all beings and carrying all beings back to the original self/the enlightened being or the original world. Just be One! *Be love!*

Happiness

This Crystal Collective All Truth is stating that "the word *happiness* is a word whose feeling is constantly being sought after. However, the happiness is already within you." You are this happiness! Bliss! Joy! You are resonating this most incredible way of being. This is the way to exist because this is who you are and nothing more. This is the only way to exist in life – the only way! The only way! When you realize that happiness is within yourself, you will be amazed.

You will realize that you are already enlightened, happy, bliss-filled, and more. When you discover yourself in the middle of a transition that you consider to be a crisis, remember that all beings are all in transition to being awakened. This is a grand shift for many – for all!

What is occurring is you are asking questions about life and all that life represents. Who am I? Where am I? What am I? How am I? It is time to shift and transition your life and it may just be in thought, emotion, Spirit, or you may just simply change the way you live your present daily life and push the *restart* button and begin again. Perhaps a new job, new relationship, new life, and more beauty. Thus determined as a transition or shift.

As the transitioning progresses through the thinning of the veil, further shifting will occur for more people. Today you may be hearing many people talking about shifting and transitioning into a new way of being and with this new way of being is also revealed the new form of soul or your sacred contract. This means you should arise to the occasion where you become filled with all that you need to become because your soul's contract is up and ready. It is up and ready to become engaged to be worked and lived through and felt. Now is your time to fulfill all that you need to fulfill.

It is time to say "now."
It is time to feel "now."
It is time to become "now."
"Now" means that you have arrived in a place that is
being considered one of joy and greatness in soul.

Within your soul's contract lives your authentic self. It always remains intact. Nothing will ever disturb your soul's contract except for you. You either accept your contract or not. You either work with who you are through your contract or not. In other words, in these times of shifting and becoming awakened or realized as to who you really are, you then begin to seek and feel your soul's contract or purpose. Of course, this is a natural occurrence and this is what one does when awakening to one's Spirit, which is bliss, joy, peace, and happiness. It is all wrapped up nicely into a large golden ball named *you*.

Why not explore who you are? Why not? More people are reading and taking courses about "Who am I? What am I? Where am I? When am I?" As you discover your authentic self you will begin to notice that all spiritual, new age, self-help/ self-growth books all say the same thing!

Be your authentic self and all of these
questions will be answered.

Watch carefully how the shifting in books on the shelves of stores becomes streamlined into one message: *You are Spirit. You are one in peace. You are stillness. You are bliss. You are Source/God. You are here to serve and accept. You are authentic.* This will be, as you can see already, the main theme or basis of all books within the self-help/self-growth, spiritual, and new age sections. These are sections that will quickly sell out their stock because they are addressing the original self. Book titles similar to, *Become Awakened, Living a Life of Stillness, Peace – You Are This!, Flow Within the Shift,* and so much more are surfacing already.

Life as you know, believe, and allow will greatly shift and become a more beautiful way of existing in the now. This is truth and as you shift, you influence others and they then shift as well.

Time becomes oblivious, illusory, and obviously unreal. Time becomes unimportant because what this means is that there is more to life than just following a watch, structure, and routine. Life has so much more to offer than this. The spiritual time is the time by which one flows and follows according to perfect plan. Spiritual time is simply a time when you become aware that there is "no time" – time is an illusion and everything that is "on time" is spiritually expressed as:

1. Living through the love of Spirit, which is self.
2. Serving and accepting love.
3. Being who you are.
4. Allowing your authentic self to stream through you.
5. Awakening to what is occurring within you and around you.

6. Living in the stillness of self, which is who you are.

7. Being and living as peace.

Therefore, *no time* and *on time* are one of the same. In other words, there is no time when in fact everything is on time. When you are feeling that everything is on time, then you don't need to worry or fret or feel anxious about anything. Because everything is on time perfectly and in fact, this is the best part, while you wait you create immediate results. Just sit and perhaps don't wait – just be seated. Don't anticipate anything. Just be still. Just *be*. This doesn't mean you don't move and sit on the couch all day unless you feel you should through your own intuition and guidance. Just be aware of flowing through your Spirit or intuition.

Your intuition/Spirit is timeless. Jump into this beautiful pool of timelessness and just allow the water to shift through you. As you flow within this pool, watch how the sun skips across the top of the pool and feel how the sun refracts its light within the pool. See how the White Light rays from the sun beam through the turquoise water to the bottom of the pool and create patterns as they are shifted through the gentle waves created by you. The sun's rays are always there and always refracting through the water, even if the waves are large. Allow the Source/the White Light shift you through the waves. These waves are just the flowing of life. They are the gentle movement of your Spirit/intuition and your feelings.

By flowing with the waves of intuition or Spirit, you then allow the warm White Light to enter every part of you. You then allow everything to shift and move through you because you really are the stillness of the water and you really are the rough tides and waves. But you are also the Light that shines through the waves and the tides. You are everything because you are Spirit.

Rise up to who you are.
Be brave, be courageous.
This is who you are!
Nothing more and nothing less but Spirit.

Get over Yourself

This next Crystal Collective All Truth is one that needs to be read with a gentle and quiet cup of golden tea or lemon water, because this message requires its own space. Space for its own processing and awakening for you. It is a message that you will carry with you *always* in *all ways* forever. It will comfort you deeply – to your core of self!

This message is one of *freedom*. If you are believing that you are locked, stuck in the middle of a crisis or a sadness, illness, depression, then stop believing this! Feel and move through it now and let it go. Get over yourself and shift into serving others. If you are experiencing sorrow, depression, crisis, and so on, push through this, and then help others who are believing they too are hopeless. So stop it, get over yourself, and get going! This is messaged in kindness for you and others. When you have freed yourself, then and only then can you assist others in a fullness from *all* of you!

This is a strong yet gentle message within these Crystal Collectives. This message is connected to all people who feel they need to remove themselves from enslaving themselves in suffering. Release the illusion of suffering and quickly choose freedom because the planet needs you now to help it and others to move out of their own suffering. This is not to say that you quit your job and become a therapist or holistic practitioner – or maybe it is! Or is it to help all people you meet on the street, in the shops, at the gas station, everywhere you go! But first free yourself!

Freedom is the releasing of everything, not just a bit of something but *everything*. You are then clearing, cleansing, and rejuvenating your old self into your new self. It is a time when the old you releases completely – not just a little bit, but completely. You will know when this point of exposure occurs. It is a point of no return. When dancing within this state of freedom, you are then within the White Light of promise, love, hope, peace, and stillness, because you see the core of stillness and love is *freedom.*

Get busy. Find that freedom, that love, that peace, that beauty, that stillness within! It is in you, you are it!

Movement of Stillness

It is here within these Crystal Collectives where all things exist and coexist. It is within this existence and coexistence whereby, according to the All Truths, the "still point" resides. It resides between the existence of who you are now and the coexistence of who you are becoming. Coexistence means the realization that you as Spirit coexist with form. Existence means to *just exist*. Therefore the individual information of existence and coexistence contained within the Crystal Collectives is now ready and available to and for you. It is ready for you to tap into and shift or transform from existing (the way you are existing now) to coexisting (the way you will exist when awakened). The "still point" is between these two events.

Since the veil is thinning between the Spirit and form, it is then becoming more accessible for humans to slide into the spiritual side or *way of being*. When this awakening occurs, all of life becomes available to you through all parts of self: the levels of body, mind, soul, Spirit, energy, and emotion. You begin to see, feel, taste, touch, and smell all things differently, and this is common when one becomes awakened. This is regular! Does this sound fantastic and wonderful? Does this sound like the way things should be? Does this sound like how life should be? It is within this recognition when all things become enwrapped with the love of Spirit and the love of Source. It is within this sense of being in Spirit where all things exist, live, and move.

All things exist and coexist with each other. This is a fact or a deep truth. In other words, Oneness of everything exists in such a way that all beings live along the Crystal Collective lines of eternity, the White Light streamed line of love.

Therefore, within the beauty of awakening or being awakened, one discovers there is so much more to *life*. As indicated above, you begin to live from a still point and this still point is a point by which all else resonates freely in life. The All Truth within this Crystal Collective also indicates that this still point is the birth point in spiritual time where awakening occurs. Living this awakened state is the life – or the "movement of stillness." In other words, when you are shifting through your day you are just taking along with you the stillness of who you are. You are just shifting from one millisecond to the next millisecond within your stillness. If you are living within that stillness or point of awakening, then this is who you are – still. But you need to walk, talk, eat, work, play, all of those ordinary everyday functions or events in life that one needs to do. Perform these regular daily life functions in stillness slowly and flowingly. Feel the flow of Spirit and your emotions moving through you, and then you respond through your mind of self or the thinker.

Therefore being or living is just and only just *movement of stillness* and nothing more. Even if you are running, biking, swimming, or walking quickly, you still are encouraged within the movement of stillness. Even if you encounter a bear, you are moving in stillness, you live in a still state and make calm and clear decisions, such as do I move away? Do I create a scene to scare the bear? Do I call for help? All of these questions are posed in a stillness and the answers arrive in stillness. This is the true form of living, which is the movement of the stillness.

The highest vibrational terms to use are movement of the stillness – moving or living through your Spirit or stillness. These terms will always remind you and cue you on a different level of existing that *you are already movement of stillness.*

Language

The term *life* is too open and meaningless now in this new place of existence. The All Truth in this Crystal Collective is indicating that "higher vibrational terms are being implemented and changing other terms that are perceived as lower vibrational terms." Lower vibrational terms are changing quickly as more people are becoming aware of the difference. The lower the vibration of the term, then the lower your vibration will go. For example, the terms *hate* and *war* have lower energetic vibration than *love* and *peace*. During these times of change, language will shift in a most dramatic and beautiful fashion. Words have energy, feeling and vibration.

Begin today to see, feel, and hear words within your language that sense to be of lower vibration and then change them to something different – that is all you do! In fact, when awakened, you will begin to sense everything differently and automatically sense words that are of lower vibration and quickly change to a higher vibration, and it is as easy as this, *once awakened!*

The All Truths are indicating that most of the human language can be rewritten to suit a vibrational energy. Isn't this an interesting concept for humans to feel? Language will indeed shift and change for all beings who have awakened. It will become finer, softer, and more tender in tone and sound, but in expression as well. How can it not become this?

As the original world prepares and transitions or approaches you, being awakened cannot just exist or move through life without shifting your language. This will automatically occur for those awakened. Those awakened will also notice a change in their thought patterns, ideas, and opinions that they never had before, therefore leading to the new forms of language. The origins of the higher language stem from being awakened to thought patterns to vocabulary. If you were to study Atlantis, the place of the crystals, you will discover that the people existing at this time communicated telepathically. The crystals are offering the suggestion that one will be able to reach such a high vibration of energy(ies) that one day you will communicate telepathically?

As stated previously in this book, the All Truths are indicating that yes, of course, there will come a time that the veil into the Spirit world is so thin that this creates an opening to further and deeper psychic abilities for all humans. Keep in mind it says that all humans are already in tune, or in the stream or psychic.

In 2012 and post-2012 more humans will become aware that their psychic abilities are heightening at a faster rate and their language usage is changing. This is an All Truth.

During the time of Atlantis, which was created by crystals, language was not necessary and healing occurred instantly within the inner workings of certain crystals. All beings living here were joined together as One through Spirit. They were considered to be living through a very pure Homo-Luminous body/form. Not unlike what is evolving now! The Crystal Collectives or the catacombs of crystals is the actual returning of Atlantis. You will begin to find people who have been reincarnated from Atlantis arriving or have arrived here on the planet in order to help out and assist in this transitioning and metamorphosis of the new world. It is here within their assistance a most wonderful way of existing will occur. It is here within their assistance where everything will be still, calm, and relaxed. They are and will be taking leadership roles in this shift – pay attention to those who are writing about the original world, speaking about it, and teaching courses about it because chances are they are beings reincarnated from Atlantis to assist each and every one of you! This is possible and in fact is truth as written or scribed.

Living from Within the Belly of Mother Earth

This All Truth from a Crystal Collective states, "One should live from the belly of Mother Earth. This is where all nurturance resides. That which is within you. The purity of life and the pleasure of Spirit!" The greenery of Mother Earth is one that is of fairness and pleasure. What this means is that the greenery is one of grandness within Mother Earth's sweetness of her belly. It is here within Mother Earth where the fairest of them all exist. The purity of life, the simplistic way of being, the slowness, and the completeness of all that is of peace exist within the belly of the mother.

It is here within the belly where you create who you are.
It is here within the belly whereby you create all that is
of love, joy, patience, graceful beingness, and elegance.
It is here within the belly of the mother whereby
lessons of fairness and pleasure are learned.
It is here within these lessons by the mother whereby all
answers to all questions are revealed and brought forward.

When one is able to contain oneself in life as a being of authentic joy or a being of the Oneness with Spirit, one then is able to contain and maintain all of the juices from life. In other words, when you are the child and then the bearer of love and peace in your life, you are then the being who is the creator of the juices of what the mother feeds you. Accept these gracious juices of life and move forward within these juices of life and rest upon all that is yours to discover. Discover all of the juices of life that are within the belly of Mother Earth. You see, she is the keeper of the reason for obtaining all that is of beauty.

These juices from the mother are your fairest qualities of who you really are: pleasure, joy, peace, gentleness, tenderness, patience, grace, and simplicity. Not unlike the events that occur in nature's growth. The events of a seed blossoming forward. When a tiny little apple seed accepts the juices from the belly of the mother, then it becomes ready to blossom forth and forward. It becomes grand in its appearance as it begins to move into its authentic being. It becomes filled with all of what life offers. This life offers many gifts to those who accept these juices of Spirit. These juices of Spirit are those that contain all of what life contains. All you need to do is tap into who you really are by allowing yourself to fully engage in all that is already within yourself. Become fully engaged in the *you*. You see, the *you* of who you are is really the belly of the mother. It is really the belly/ the inner part of who you are. It is the Essence of your being because you are that belly of Mother Earth. When you were in fetus state, you were in the belly of the mother – her Spirit or her juices of nurturance, her soil, her life, her Godliness, and so on. You were there being grown or raised by the invisible Source to a point where it was now your turn to push through her belly to see and meet the sun, and it is here within this Source where you discover freedom.

Each being is created and born free, free for surrendering yourself to the God/Source/White Light. What this means is the following: why would you freeze up in fear, anxiety, and worry when you are already created from God/Source? Why would you become filled with worry, fear, and anger when in fact you are that simple flower that has poked itself out of the belly of the Mother and lives a very beautiful, carefree, loving, peace-filled, still life! Why would you believe the thoughts of ego and even rest comfortably with these thoughts?

See how upside down this can be? When born, you are freshly made like a beautiful loaf of homemade warm bread. You are fully engaged in the juices of Spirit. You have no doubt that you are Spirit now in human form. No doubt in the world much like or rather exactly like a newborn flower. This newborn flower has no doubt in its petals that it is Spirit as it drinks from its juices of life. You see, the only difference between a newborn fetus and the newborn flower is that an ego of negative thoughts tries to influence the newborn fetus. As he/she grows, he/she hears, feels, tastes, and touches that which resonates from the ego of others not himself/herself but others. As parents, words arriving such as *be careful, don't do this, don't do that, you can't do this, you can't do that, oh dear you must be tired,* etc. This is information being programmed into you to create excuses to not fulfill your fullness of life, soul's purpose, or authentic self when an adult. Yes, an adult. You see, when as a child you are vulnerable, open, simple, peace-filled, creative, and trusting. You believe what you are told by your parents so that when you are an adult you begin to live your life feeling, believing, and knowing the programmed ideas. For example, if you were told "Don't do this, you are too tired!" then from this belief perhaps as an adult you still believe that maybe you are "too tired" to do this or that and therefore this belief resonates throughout your entire self and, perhaps sadly, your entire life.

See how much influence parents have with their children? However, remember now that you are an adult and it is time for you to collect yourself and grow up. Grow up into being that beauty within the flower. That genuine Essence! The Essence that is the Source. This is who you really are! You are not what you were told who you are by anybody! The telling of who you are came from parents who were also told the same by their parents and so on and so forth. Allow yourself to become completely aware of what is happening here for you. You as the reader need to know, feel, and believe the importance of the Source within you. What this means is the wisdom that is within you and that you need to tap into – that is all. Allow yourself the wisdom to be exposed to the White Light force. You were created by the mother's juices of Spirits, which is God/White Light/Source. Now is your time to really believe this! Know this! Feel this! Allow this! And let go!

It is believed that now is a most crucial time in our history. It is a time when all beings are made aware of their Spirit in one form or another. Prepare yourself for this point of choice. Once you are aware of this point or choice, you then become aware of all that is occurring on this planet. Patience is a grand virtue and being still and peaceful is the core of one's existence. You see, within the core of the stillness is peace and the grandeur feeling of this and nothing more.

Begin to take note of everything around you. Begin to become aware of all of life and its messages and promises. These are the times or spaces or gaps in life when all decisions are made. These are the times or spaces where many grand decisions will be made and many great spiritual ideas will be exchanged. This is truth. Arrive then in this place of allowing. Comfort yourself in this allowing and awaken to who you really are. It is a knowing!

Retreat

Within the cavities of this Crystal Collective is the All Truth message about *retreat*. Retreating means moving into self. Perhaps you are being drawn to go someplace – this may mean a sacred temple, a room in your home, another country, a garden walk, a mountain hike, a restaurant, or even moving into you more deeply. Pay attention to this feeling of *retreat* and move with this feeling of *just being* or *retreat*. It means that Spirit has a message for you! When engaged within this knowing, it is then wise to follow it and see, feel, hear, taste, and touch where it goes. Move with the flow of what you feel you know – nothing more than this! When you are feeling like you are being called to be someplace or somewhere then it is important to be there. Go! Don't analyze it – just go! Don't make it complicated – just go! Within this space, it may be your time to experience that point of awakening or deep awakenings. It may be a time in space whereby you will discover that which is what you are looking for.

Pay attention to everything that is going on around you! It may be within the mystery of the moment of where you are that you find the solstice of life, that peace and stillness you have been seeking. These terms *retreat* or *just be* are one and the same. Retreating to just be – retreat and retreat and retreat yourself into just being the *isness* of self that is the Spirit within. This is called the evolution of Spirit. Human beings, at least most of them, require the need to evolve slowly into anything! Because change can be quite difficult for most. This gentle evolution is required in order for the shifting and the reconfiguration to occur. This shifting and reconfiguration are required in order for the awakening to happen. That point of awakening is most vital and must not be taken lightly. Or should it be taken lightly? Within this place of retreat – really anywhere you decide to go or are drawn to – remember that you have a most amazing and beautiful gifted message coming your way. It is here within the message that you shall experience the point of awakening. When you do feel this point of awakening, it then opens the door to your retreat so that you will have access to the "just is" sacred room or retreat that has been perfectly prepared just for you and only you.

Your sacred retreat room of *just is* is the *isness* energy of being who you are. That authentic way of being – the way to exist, the only way to exist and participate in this life. When one recognizes that one is already filled with the Spirit of love, light, and joy – you are then able to shift and move into a great place filled with sunshine, gardens, moonbeams, starlight, warm breezes, and more – this is your retreat! This is your place of stay – your isness, your way of being. It is this and nothing more than this! It *is just is.*

The Energy of Money

Around the corner of 2012 is 2013, and within this year of 2013 and beyond, humans will realize that money will be changing its energy and abundance. There will be a whole new way of viewing and feeling the energy of money. It will be considered as meaningless and in some cases useless – this is from a spiritual perspective!

In other words, serving and receiving or accepting will inevitably have more meaning from a spiritual perspective than a financial perspective. What this means according to the All Truths in this Crystal Collective is that "as humans evolve spiritually, their *spiritual connection* to the planet and others is more valuable than the tangible form of money." Money will still be used as an exchange form but will no longer be the necessity because humans will begin to serve each other from the heart, soul, and Spirit, not simply for money but for spiritual receiving and giving.

This has several implications for the financial institutions of the world. What will occur post-2012 is the financial institutions will align and realign in order to provide money and abundance to all people – poverty will be examined fully from larger financial institutions. The Essence of Spirit will insert itself in the institutions of finances. Remember too that as more and more people become awakened, then more people understand the energy of money and how it has shifted.

The energy of money will shift to a different level of vibration, meaning a higher vibration in order to match Spirit. Presently, for many humans the energy of money is a lower vibration and the ego picks up on this and then greed begins to occur, relationships are dismantled, and even companies are dissolved. However, because of the shift of energies with the planet, the concept of money will also shift for the better. As stated, people will no longer worry about the abundance of money and the loss of money because the primary focus is upon Spirit and how to serve. This does not mean that money will be no longer needed (however by 3012 this will indeed be the case), but it just means it will be looked upon differently. This also doesn't mean that abundance will not be flowing. In fact, abundance will be in full force in terms of money, love, peace, stillness, soul, relationships, bliss and/or pure happiness, and so on. This abundance and more will be accepted in all ways as one manifests what one needs immediately.

To clarify, money will be available and lots of it, but this will not have the same meaning as before because of the awakening of self. Money will lend itself to being meaningless, irrelevant, and useless because the ego will no longer require this form of energy because the ego will no longer be fed. When the ego isn't fed, greed, pain, suffering, and the needing of more money begin to become less of a worry. And really it is just an energy form that simply shifts back and forth. This is not saying that it won't be appreciated, it will just no longer be the central focus of people's lives – that is all! Because the focus will be how they live within their awakened state. Remember that all people will be taken care of, without question!

Simplicity as a Boat

This Crystal Collective is one that messages the All Truths concerning "simplicity." *Simplicity* involves a way of being, existing, feeling, thinking, and speaking. It is the way of existing within the world on this planet in an easy manner that depicts a life without worries, fears, anxieties, confusions, war, and hatred. What this is indicating is that when one becomes awakened, one begins to realize how simple and easy life is when one begins to see, feel and know that if a perceived crisis occurs that there is a spiritual and beautiful reason for its occurrence. You may feel its pain, fear, and/or anger and then move forward in life. You do not get stuck or attached in these feelings because you know that this occurrence or event has happened for a reason connected to Spirit. This is just one example of *simplicity*.

You move through perceived crisis with grace and a knowing that everything will be perfect and is in perfect order. You are grounded in Spirit, which means you resonate love and stillness in a real way, not in an ungrounded way. When grounded within your emotions of Spirit, you begin to have an easier life and everything seems not so complicated because you have awakened to a new state of being.

You recognize that conflicts between you and others have lessened, and, if they occur, you handle them differently because you now know that you can't take this personally and you will handle this in grace. You don't need to analyze every single detail of everything about the conflict because you understand something differently. What you have done is *let go*. You have stated that you are letting go and letting God/Source shine through you. This makes everything so much easier in life. You are then declaring that you are the boat with the gracefully designed sails and Spirit is the wind. I will turn my boat into the stream of wind every single time because it is easier to have the wind of Spirit blow my sails than me struggling to paddle against the wind. It is just easier and the wind knows where I should go and I know that the wind knows. I believe in the wind of Spirit and I allow the wind of Spirit to fill my sails. My intention is *knowing, believing,* and *allowing* the wind of Spirit to place me in the perfect position in life. My only job is to tend to my boat – wash it, shine it, fix it, and care deeply for it. You see, my body or form is the boat or the vessel that needs to be tenderly cared for in order for the winds to smoothly move my sails or for Source to work through me.

Life is very simple.

Lifted by Spirit

This message as energetically scribed in the All Truth within this Crystal Collective contains one of the most incredible realizations you can experience when awakened. The All Truth realization that, when awakened you are actually being lifted extremely high in Spirit and energy and what this means is that you are able to feel this sensation of being *lifted*. This feeling may be sensed differently by different people. Some may feel this sensation above their heads, others out from the solar plexus (abdominals), and for some the heart. What this sensation feels like is a large warm ball of energy that is soft in form and intense in love, peace, joy, stillness, and bliss. When you are able to discover this ball of energy, you then are able to move into this ball of energy and allow this ball to relax and calm you into a state of complete relaxation. A deep knowing that everything is wonderful. No matter what. This *everything* is the *beginning* of *everything* and *anything* for you when awakened.

When you feel this place of lightness you are then able to shift and move into this place in a most wonderful and beautiful way. This shifting is a way in which you become engaged in sensing everything around you. This feeling of the beauty of being lifted is a most sacred feeling. When you discover this ball of energy you may even hear certain forms of music, smell a certain incense, taste a certain smell, or even hear words of love. You may even feel an angelic touch on your shoulder or any other part of your body. When awakened, realizations occur rapidly and surely. This realization is one of the most amazing and confirming realizations you could possibly have because it is so tangible. It is an energy ball that you can feel and enter.

Life of Transparency

Think is next All Truth scribed within this Crystal Collective is one that will guide you into feeling and living a life of transparency. When you become aligned in being awakened, you then move into an existence of feeling and *seeing* transparency. All is see-through. All is clear and easy. All is actually benign – not ill or dis-eased but clear, pure, and transparent. The transparency is the Spirit that gleams or shines through the form that becomes the transparent unmanifested. Meaning what? Meaning as the veil thins or the form or body, thins, Source is able to shine or gleam forth through the form or body, thus allowing the form to become transparent and formless.

Form and all forms are becoming formless, which means that as you awaken to your Spirit within self you become attuned to all that occurs around, through, and within you. Your form (body) then slowly becomes formless because you are being guided, not manipulated into Spirit. Transparency begins to occur at that still point of decision to be awakened. When awakened, you then begin to transform into a transparent life and then life becomes transparent or apparent to you very quickly and easily. You become attuned to all of life and all that it truly is.

Transparency is truth and truth is transparency – that is all! That is the reality when one is awakened. As you become or transform into the Homo-Luminous form or energy body you are considered formless or Spirit filled to the point where you are completely still and silent!

You become so attuned to everything that is going on around and within you that you move or shift through life in a very transparent, easeful way – slowly, peacefully, still, and One with all. When one is transparent and others are as well then conflicts are resolved swiftly and lovingly. Eventually conflicts, anxieties and worries will not exist because everything is transparent. War will become an old used-up term and action. This All Truth states:

"When awakened, everything becomes transparent
within the Oneness of Source/Spirit.
When awakened, you are then officially transparent.
When awakened, you become attuned to all of
nature and nature becomes attuned to you.
When awakened, you live as peace!"

Transparency is being clear, clean, true, open, and still-filled or peaceful. And when you are living like this, then the universe will say, "I will give you more of this sweet child. I give you more of what you are thinking and feeling." And so be it!

Soul's Purpose

This Crystal Collective's All Truth states that "soul's purpose is love or the awakened self." It means to serve others through this Essence of love. All beings are all One – there is no one special being. All are equal. Nature knows this without question. Nature knows that the love of survival is all there is. So what does this mean? Nature loves to survive in a life form and in Spirit form. Humans are now just beginning to feel this feeling of the love to live in Spirit within the human form. Yes, of course plants are Spirit beings too. They feel your energy, hear you speak, sense your touch – they are Spirit in form! Form of tree, tulips, blades of grass, weeds, and pea pods.

The soul's purpose, meaning feeling love of self and giving this love to others, may resonate differently with each person. Perhaps one human being knows, feels, and believes his/her love will be placed into a passion concerning nature and being with nature but still exuding that love to others and everything about life. But taking some special *love attention* or passion or the harmony of the song they wish to sing to nature. This doesn't mean they don't sing for others! They just know, feel, and believe that the harmony of their song is for nature and therefore creating an orchestra of love – named "Soul's Purpose for and to Nature." This in no way means, according to the All Truths, that you choose who you give love to – or who you serve.

Here is the best part of the purpose of soul: to love is "when you love nature passionately, you are still loving all beings because nature is One with all." If your love transforms into a passion for art, then the energy of the love will be implanted into the art for all to feel and absorb this love energy. The All Truths could even change the term *soul's purpose* to the following words: "the purpose of your soul is to love all beings." Your passion will surface from this love and this is one way you will express the love of your soul to others.

Discover and open your entire being to who you really are and you will discover that a soul's purpose is only living through love. Tightly woven in love are bliss, stillness, and Essence. All three of these are who you already are. One just needs to come to the realization that this is you – simple!

Soul = Spirit = Oneness is "love" = Soul's Purpose

Pacing of Awakening

This Crystal Collective's All Truth surrounds the piece/ peace of you that requires *pacing*. When you have awakened, it is vital that you pace your life in solid grounded footsteps. You arrive in a place of awakening through the *pacing* of the universe. Then you pace your life and allow the awakening of self to lead you through a slow reshifting and reshaping of who you really are.

What this inevitably means is that along the crystal line of eternity of all Spirits, the pacing of awakening is gently and ever so carefully placed. The pacing of each and every single awakened person is slow and careful – this is in perfect order. If all people awaken at the same time, it will break the energy system and the vibrations would overload.

This means one person at a time or small or large groups are being awakened bit by bit and this is planned. If the whole world awakened, there would exist too much confusion and ungrounded-ness. This way, as people are slowly being awakened, they are then tenderly reshaping and reshifting their lives according to their awakened state. Their awakened state is what drives their being. Therefore these transformations should occur slowly. Reshaping is a form of coming back to who you really are and welcoming that being and allowing that Spirit to move and work through you in a most beautiful way. You are that instrument of peace. You are that tool of love.

Gently the Source is pacing for people to awaken. Think and feel it this way: how do you feel when you are jarred from a deep sleep by a loud bell or alarm clock versus classical soft music? Source is playing soft classical music for you to awaken yourself and for you to begin to ease into this most beautiful classical arrangement of music as one of the instruments of peace. Easily, gently, letting go and just being!

Crumbling of Wisdom

This Crystal Collective All Truth's message stems from the scribed energetic information from the scrolled inner core of the collective named *wisdom*. The information buried within this particular Crystal Collective is information that is considered to be of extremely high vibrational frequency and is directly connected to wisdom. Wisdom that was required throughout the ages was indeed necessary in order for this spiritual evolution to occur. It is here within this evolution of knowledge or wisdom whereby all things will crumble. This means the *crumbling* of the wisdom and knowledge becomes the next or perhaps the final piece of wisdom so declared by human and Spirit! What does this mean? It means that all wisdoms and knowledge(s) will be no longer relevant and available. The old knowledge and the old wisdom of society, spirituality, science, technology, health, life, and more will no longer be valid. This All Truth is indicating that "the new wisdom or the *wisdom of origin* is this: Spirit. All wisdom or knowledge is based upon Spirit."

In fact this All Truth is stating there are *points of amnesia* upon the planet. These points of amnesia indicate that the information concerning specific events will never be revealed. One point of amnesia is the creation of the human body. Several people have spent millions of dollars trying to uncover the secret of supposed evolution – this information will never be revealed. It is closed off energetically. Another point of amnesia is the memory of transitioning from Source into the human body. Again this memory will never be revealed and is closed off energetically. The Spirit is saying all is love. Move your life into Spirit. All is complete.

Spirit *just is* – nothing more. There are no secrets and no inner cavities that one must travel to in order to achieve isness. Truly in this sense of the word there is no more wisdom related to research, mysticism of symbols, books, secrets of cave documents, and more. Now that we are approaching the origin of the planet, one needs to dissolve the word wisdom, which is exactly what the energy scripted messages are saying – nothing!

The wisdom has evolved to nothing, meaning *all is now complete*. There is nothing more to say specifically about this term called wisdom because it no longer exists. This term has always implied "known by only a few!" This term was given to those who were able to prophesize: religious and/or spiritual teachers, prophets, masters of Spirit (now ascended, such as Jesus), and so on. However, everything is evolving spiritually and now there is no need for the term wisdom because all information or all feelings of origin are available to all. These feelings of love, stillness, joy, grace, and elegance are feelings where everything resides. It is here within this place that all information (if you so desire to call Spirit information) is provided.

Therefore all informed beings are those living without information but *in-form* means to be *in form* and not be in-Spirit or inspired. Those who need to be *in-formed* first will be considered as requiring written and/or spoken information, then they will decide upon living in-Spirit or inspired. They need to depend upon those others (authors, speakers, and those living an in-Spirit life) before they believe it all to be real. Meaning Spirit!

These humans requiring information, wisdoms, and knowledge are in fact missing the point! The point at which you feel your Spirit, your Essence, your stillness, is actually *the point!* Nothing more! In fact, your entire life can be built upon and created from and realized from this point! It takes just one second or less to feel this point – this point in feeling your Essence can and will change you forever.

You don't need to read anything, go anywhere, do anything, take a course, or travel to India – it can, if you choose, occur this very second as you sit on your favorite couch or chair. It is as simple as this! No inner deep wisdom needs to occur because it is already within. Just feel – that is all! And don't be afraid. Just allow, believe, and know. It is within the knowing or a feeling whereby everything resides. This is it!

Old Thought and Behavior Patterns

These collectives are messaging as an All Truth that when "one has become awakened, you begin to see and feel your patterns of behaviors, thoughts, and feelings." You begin to realize that who you were before being awakened is no longer relevant and that you are now seeing through the transparencies of life and how this shifts and changes. You see and feel old, dysfunctional or complex behavior, emotional patterns, and thought patterns, and you shift and change them into beautiful new patterns. You see, these old patterns are patterns or programs that you believe as real and in fact they are not. For example, believing that you are only worthy of a partner who is abusive and unkind to you because this is what you have allowed yourself to always believe. When awakened, these old belief patterns melt away quickly because you are now seeing everything more clearly and concisely.

When old patterns break away or dissolve, new beautiful ideas, thoughts, and feelings, fill these empty spaces of old broken patterns. These spaces become filled with love, bliss, peace, stillness, grace, passion, and compassion. These spaces then are awakened to Spirit. You will notice that all of the spaces within you, whether filled with old patterns or not, will become filled with awakened Spirits.

Walk into this particular day or evening watching carefully for spaces that need to be filled with an awakened Spirit.

Moving Through the Details in Life

Be clearly aware of the way in which you move and shift through life. This movement and shifting is that which makes you aware of what is going on and what is happening in every detail of life. These details in life may be the most important details for and to you. Recognize that each detail of life has a specific message for you. For example, the clouds you view in the open blue-gray sky have details of swooshing, soft, and fluffy pieces. The tree leaves have details of wee tiny veins within their skin that supply these leaves with their food – have you noticed?

Have you noticed how a bird plays with the winds and allows the wind tunnels to move it throughout the skies? Have you truly noticed the details of life? For this is the next layer of being awakened. The message from the All Truths in this Crystal Collective is "noticing details in all of life." Notice even the tiny scrawny legs of a spider or the strong bony legs of a spider crab near the ocean floor. Notice how inch by inch a bean sprout pokes its wondrous head through Mother Earth's belly! Have you felt and noticed the nature Spirits within all of nature?

Have you felt and noticed the feeling of the belly of the Mother as you lie on top of her – feel the warm red Spirit or energy move into your belly. Feel and notice Father Sky beaming down upon you and through you. For this just *noticing and feeling* is the All Truth coming through the Crystal Collectives.

When awakened or beginning to awaken,
just sit back and notice!
Notice everything and feel everything!

Attachment

This Crystal Collective's All Truth scribed message involves the "programmed mind, attachment, and non-attachment." When awakened to who you are you begin to feel, see, and notice what you are attached to and what you are not attached to and this attachment has been described by several authors, spiritual leaders, and others. But what one needs to also know is that attachment will melt off you when you have awakened. You begin to realize it immediately and you shed all things and all ideas, thoughts, feelings, and opinions with gladness in Spirit. What this inevitably means is that you open yourself up to the possibility that life can be led without attachments.

You may discover that you are attached to objects, certain emotions, relationships in a co-dependent manner, a job that may no longer suit you, and possibly more. This All Truth is indicating that "attachment is solely based upon fear, and fear alone." If you were to believe that you can't part with that old grandfather chair in the corner of the room that nobody ever uses, by the way, this is just fear! If you think, believe, and feel that if your relationship with your husband, wife, or partner dismantled that you would then be nobody – this is fear. Both of these examples of attachment are controlled and led only by fear. So how did you acquire this fear?

This fear is simply an illusion dictating to you that somehow you won't be able to cope in life if you let go of the chair and give it away to an agency, school, or family. Or if you find yourself shifting through a divorce, your fear may state "you can't cope." These two examples are common for attachments to items and/or relationships. These fears have been programmed into yourself since you were a child. Perhaps you sensed your parents' fears within their own attachment difficulties. Perhaps you went through a divorce as a child and saw and felt the fear. Therefore you became programmed to never allow this to happen to you ever. If you are a parent, be careful and gentle upon your children because every single thing you say, feel, taste, touch, watch, and more your children are absorbing completely. As an adult now today, look at your life! Are you still attached by fear?

All attachments are bound by the glue of fear. When one becomes awakened, then one is able to put some very interesting pieces together. You are able to clearly see, feel, and hear using all of your senses the attachments that you are still allowing to run your life.

Even if you lost your great grandmother's wedding ring, you will have no emotional or material attachment pop up. You will only feel and think, *Well I guess it was time for her to go. If the ring is to show up one day, that is okay, and if not, that is okay too.* You see the difference between creating a dramatic scene versus letting go and letting God. Do you feel the difference between the ego *suffering* ("What are you now going to do without the ring? It was worth a lot of money.") and the grace of *letting go* ("I let you go if you need to go.").

When awakened and living in this place of now you begin to see and feel these programmed fears and the results being attached. When you realize within your awakening that you are Spirit/Source/God/peace/bliss and more, you then realize that fear is not included. You no longer need to live through fear. This is no longer necessary because it is not who or what you are. You are the purity of love and Spirit – not fear. Where there is love, there is no fear, and where there is fear, there is no love – that's it. Nothing more!

Release your fears and allow attachments to melt away because you are safe and you are completely safe.

Reality Changes

Within this Crystal Collective is the All Truth information based upon the inner dialogue of Source and the human, that being the *dimension of reality*. What this means is that your dimension of reality is now different from before. As stated, within this All Truth, your reality changes as you change your reality. This means you are the one to change your life. You, as the human form, need a dialogue with Spirit about your reality, but this dialogue is not so much talking but *feeling*.

When you have this inner feeling dialogue between you and Spirit, you begin to see a whole new reality or life right before your eyes. And in fact your third eye begins to open and see more clearly. You begin to experience life from a different place in space – a place from a stillness and nothing more than that, as stated several times – this then is the place of reality for all people. For one who chooses to live from this place will become a different person. When you become awakened, your third eye – that energy center between your eyes on your forehead – becomes awakened and alive. You begin to see all things more clearly. You begin to see things from the perspective of Spirit. You open yourself up more in order to see more – this is what happens! All becomes clearer and all rejuvenates itself. You become engaged in life and filled with joy.

Your Own Personal Crystals

Within this Crystal Collective is information regarding your *own personal crystals* through the All Truths. The crystals are actually within your cells – each cell within your entire body has a tiny crystal in energy form. Each and every tiny single crystal is filled with Sourceful/ White Light information. Wrapped within this information is the rainbow crystal healing energy. Just as the sun shining through a crystal creates the rainbow, the reflection of the White Light through your personal crystals creates the healing crystal rainbow energy within you. This healing rainbow energy is the new energy that is being revealed through your crystals. As you recognize or are awakened to your true self, One with Spirit, it follows that by eating foods from the sun further opens the messages within the rainbow energy. Once the crystals have been activated, their energy information is then released. In other words, when you begin to realize that you are Spirit in human form, then the crystals start to activate and open. They begin to release the necessary messages and this downloading is one of greatness of heart. It defines all of what life or moving in stillness is and will be.

These messages from the crystals within you are the same information that is being messaged from the catacombs of crystals within the earth's energy. It is the same information that is embedded within Mother Nature and Father Sky. The same!

Each little being has this crystal or crystallized information available to him/her. Even the itty-bitty petal on the tiniest flower has this information. It is here within this information where all things are revealed.

When you have been awakened, all of the crystals then activate and open up or download their information to you – which are the mystic laws or the All Truths. When this occurs, everything becomes clear – it truly is an *ah ha* moment or a state of I now get it or I now see what is going on here. It is within this ah ha or *I now get it* whereby a full peace-filled state occurs or the stillness makes itself known. This makes sense and pulls everything together because, as stated earlier, these All Truths or mystic laws (old term) are within all people and available to all people, not just a few people called *mystics*. This would also account for why it feels so wonderful, comfortable, and still to all people when hiking in the forest, on a mountain, or even in your backyard garden because nature and you, have the same Crystal Collective information – all are mystics. Therefore you are feeling nature's energies or Spirits of these crystals.

Even when a tree falls in the forest through disease or otherwise, its crystals still remain intact until it decays. Then the crystals just simply enter the belly of Mother Earth or the soil and refresh the earthen rock with its message of stillness. When this occurs, it then becomes the crystal or the circle of Oneness – the new form of describing the now – a circle. This Oneness then is of the crystals, energy, Spirit, and all beings of Source. You see how this works? Everything is connected to everything. Humans are Spirits and so are the grasses, trees, flowers, sea life, birds, insects, spiders, and all animals. All are connected through the Crystal Collectives within each and every cell. This is truth!

This also explains why human beings love being in nature or even just viewing nature, because the largest piece/peace of them is connected in an extraordinary way – through the energy of the crystals. It is here within these crystals where everything is revealed. You just need to activate them by beginning to realize they are there and this is you!

When realizing this above All Truth, you begin to look at everything in life differently. You begin to see, feel, hear, touch, taste, and even smell life differently because it is different – it is so connected to Spirit you will be amazed. Realize then that everything of nature and humans are connected. That is all. This is the Oneness that is the main thread throughout this book.

Water

The human form is held together by only the energy of water. This Crystal Collective's All Truth states, "this energy of water is composed of crystals and these crystals are the make-up of all water molecules." Each molecule is composed of these crystals and within the crystals is the rainbow energy. Therefore the composition of each water molecule within the self of your form is a collection of crystals. These crystals take on different shapes and forms according to your vibrational stance or the amount of light passing through your crystals. So be open to the full spectrum of light.

The higher your vibration, the clearer your crystal messages or All Truths are and the crisper the information will be wrapped throughout love. This Crystal Collective of All Truths is then woven around your full form of self. In other words, this then becomes a way of being and existing. The crystals within the molecules of the water cells are defined by the way the Crystal Collectives have been created. They, the Crystal Collectives, are wrapped within or scribed through or scrolled within the Crystal Palace, which is built upon the All Truths or mystic laws.

These laws or truths are scrolled or scribed within these Crystal Collectives, which are stationed within your form and sustained within the water molecules. Remember that these water molecules make up 95 to 99 percent of your form, thus water from the sea, sky, earth, air, fire (fire creates the mist or the beauty of condensation), and ether. Ether is the Spirit that is the flow of energy or the composition of all that needs to occur in order for you as Spirit to enter the form.

In other words, in order for the Spirit to enter the form/ the material body, it needs to attach to the crystal molecules of the water droplets within the form. The Spirit is therefore in all beings because all human beings are mainly water molecules, so even if a spiritual trickle is seen within a person who is filled with fear and anger, it is okay because the crystallized molecules of the water are still holding and maintaining the Spirit in place. The Spirit never leaves until the transition out of the body or form.

Wouldn't it be interesting to compare the water molecules of crystals of a person who is living and believing in fear, hate, self-sabotage, or anger to a person who is living and believing in love, joy, peace, stillness, and passion? The book *The Hidden Messages in Water,* by Masaru Emoto (Emoto, Masaru. *The Hidden Messages in Water.* Carlsbad, CA. Hay House Publishing. 2005.) examined the actual water molecules of water droplets from a variety of water sources throughout the planet. Emoto discovered that each of these molecules is different and each design of these molecules matches directly the energetic vibration of the place/city/ county. In other words, in a country that has been through war and continues to create more war, the crystals or the designs of the water molecules are broken and not in the purest form or design. The places where the energetic vibration is high or finer in vibration, the molecules of the water as designed by the crystals are in absolute perfect form.

As stated in many sections within this *Movement of Stillness* book, the Crystal Collectives All Truths are placed and stationed throughout your entire self and all of nature and this is why everything is based upon water. You cannot live without the absorption of water. You will dry up your crystal molecules of the water crystals. In other words, your crystals will dry up and crackle. You will create a brittle way of being and this is defined by ego. Ego wants the moisture out of your form/your body. It wants you to be stiff, raw, and brittle. But the Spirit and the perfect design or the natural creation of the crystallized water molecules are moist, fluid, crystal clear in high vibration, and in the fullest of love.

Isn't this most fascinating? When you take care of your body, you then are taking care of the crystals as wrapped around the water molecules. They become fully wrapped around their high vibrational energetic form and therefore transmit the messages as being moved through you in a very crystal-clear fashion. Your Spirit and the other White Light Spirits, through other dimensions, are then able to move through you at an enormous speed. The speed of love. The speed of enlightenment. This speed of love/speed of light is the speed at which all messages move through you to others.

As you rearrange the way you exist through being awakened to the fact that you are already an enlightened being, you then begin to rebuild your Crystal Collective part of who you truly are through the water molecules. These crystal pieces then rebuild and their edges become clearer. Their messages open up and, *voila,* the crystal opens and the All Truths or the realizations reveal themselves to you.

What this means is that when you awaken to the realization that you are already an enlightened being, then immediately the Crystal Collectives within your water molecules open up and speak to and through you. You begin to see, feel, hear, and sense everything differently or crystal clear! You realize other realizations that occur throughout your world and your life. You realize that everything is just within yourself and no place outside yourself. However, you should also realize that the crystal information is outside yourself as well as maintained through the energy packages or the crystal scrolls. In other words, the crystal molecules exist in nature through the water molecules. Everything in nature has a water molecule attached.

In review, open yourself up to the possibility that you are filled with the crystals as intertwined within the water molecules. You have the opportunity to access this information whenever you wish to because this is who you are. When awakened, you fully open up the crystal All Truths messages. This then exposes the true pieces of who you are. This is the way you can live and be as the isness of being. This is who you are *being* – just being who you truly are – *the crystal molecules of self.* You are the mineralized crystals as depicted within the water molecules. Nothing more!

Vibrations of Nature

The Crystal Collectives of this All Truth is a message surrounding the messages that are contained within and throughout the winds, the bird's song verses of peace and joy, the chirps of the insects, and the rustling of the grass as the rabbit skips through its tickling touch. All messages are contained, remain, and are mentioned within the nature of all of life, from the winds to the insects to the stones and crystals of messages. All messages are wound around each Spirit of nature and within and around its vibrational message. The vibration that is exuded by each Spirit of Nature is an important message. To explain further, when a nature Spirit releases its messages and gifts, it will be of pure form of feeling, touch, words, and song to each person who is open to accepting its message.

Many people are now able to channel not only into White Light Spirits but also Spirits of nature. Some humans can and will communicate to you what the tree Spirit and its being are saying to you directly. They may also be able to channel information as conveyed by the Spirit of the flower, blade of grass and leaf of a mountain tree.

The vibration from the Spirits of nature may then be also *felt*. This vibration is the energy and its messages through feeling. In other words, visualize the following: a beautiful sunset setting in the west and you suddenly *feel* tranquility, peacefulness, stillness, and grace. *This* is the vibrational message. It is here within the feeling message where you are able to transform the feeling into a verbal word message. It is here within this transformation, where clarity settles in. It is here within the feeling that the verbal or other form of message is revealed. It is within these messages one is able to feel, see, hear, touch all this, what life is truly about – tranquility, peace, stillness, grace, love, and joy.

These feelings are always channeled directly to and for you. All for you to become strongly connected to Spirit, which is you. You don't need to be awakened to see, feel, touch, or hear a sunset – it just is – it just exists and you see the tranquility, feel the peace, touch the stillness, and hear the grace. This is all that is being communicated and all of this is the channeled feelings or messages as gifted to you just from one single sunset.

Next time you are hiking or strolling gently through nature, what do you feel, hear, touch, smell, and taste? These messages of All Truths from the Crystal Collectives are intertwined within all of nature because all of nature is composed of these tiny Crystal Collectives.

Place of Completeness

The All Truth within this Crystal Collective is saying, "You don't have to go anywhere to find out that what you are seeking is already within *you*." Nowhere else but that which is within you is you! You are that one being, that Spirit of beauty. This would be you. You are this and you are that!

It really is as simple as this. This is really all what you need to know in terms of everything. Your core is Spirit and it is within this recognition where you become fully awakened and alive in this knowing. This knowing is exactly that knowing. You then say, "I know that I am Spirit. *I know* that I am who I am, which is of course Spirit and all that it represents. The knowing is the Spirit saying to you, "Here I am. This is who I am – Spirit – and you are just simply knowing this!"

The All Truth Crystal Collectives are saying that when you know, you then live a very different way of being. You live a life of freedom and a life filled with amazement. It is here within this amazement when your whole life begins. It begins with you becoming more attuned to what is happening around you. It begins with you believing that everything is absolutely perfect and then living and existing within this place and time. This place is a comfortable place and just requires you knowing it – that's all!

Be One of Beauty in Everything You Do

This Crystal Collective is one that messages from the All Truths that all "are Oneness in love." As you become more awakened to who you are, you then begin to feel the *Hallelujah* chorus of the Divine presence within you and all of those around you. You become filled with a realization that all beings and all of nature are One with you and One with all that you require and need to acquire. Be of beauty in all that is of yourself.

Continue to maintain that which is truly who you are. You are this as is all of nature. All of nature will be drawn to you and for you because nature will feel and recognize that you are now awakened. As you shift and move through your day you will notice nature all around you even if you are located in a large, busy, loud city. You will notice, feel, touch, smell, and taste nature even if you see a small flower or grass peeking up from the corner of a piece of pavement. This peeking up from the pavement is symbolic that even through some difficult times, a shining new flower or piece of hope will pop-up no matter what.

When one is living in an awakened state, one then begins to know, believe, and allow oneself to move through these believed or perceived states of difficult times in one smooth movement not unlike a serpent shedding its skin. As it does, a birthing, a newness, and a revitalization occurs, and a newfound way of existing in life.

As you move deeply into your awakened state of being, you will connect intensely to yourself. You then begin to see difficult times or moments filled with purpose or reason. This is why you are able to pop-up out of an ego-based state of suffering because, you are awakened to a higher purpose. When existing or living in a deepened state of awakening, you then are able to see, feel, hear, touch, taste, and even smell a perceived crisis arriving around the corner – it's called intuition. What occurs is that you evolve into such a spiritual state of being awakened that you get to know the feeling of something arriving that may be interpreted as crisis, darkness or trauma. This is not so uncommon. For example, a woman or a man discovers his/her partner is having an affair with another person and they would say, "I knew it." Or an executive of a company is told, "Your company is going to close" and she/he says, "I knew this would occur."

The meaning of all that occurs in life is *stilled* or is *placed in a space* for confrontation of what is inside of yourself and what is the inner knowing of who you are. In other words, what just happened, you already knew would happen, and now it is your time to explore deeply within. Deep within yourself, that needs to be further awakened, which is what your Spirit is wanting so much for you to do. Awaken to a deeper level – listen to it! This does not mean that when you deeply awaken to the core of who you are that you may not face or feel hurt, pain, or fear. The difference is that you will not only move through these feelings faster but also will *know* everything is in perfect plan and order. You will be so plugged into Spirit – yourself – that you will know at such a visceral level that you can't help but know.

Your sixth sense develops quickly and intensely when you have awakened to your Spirit state of being. This is the realized state of existence. One of beauty and love! It is here where all is kept and all is known. It is throughout your entire self, your heart, solar plexus (abdominals), legs, arms, mind, and all parts of physical and emotional knowing! This visceral level of such deep and intense knowing means that you are able to make decisions quickly, accurately, and assuredly – not questions, but decisions made in a blink! You just know exactly what to do – it is a feeling.

For example, perhaps as the man or woman of the partner who had the affair you knew years ago or even the day of the wedding (couple ceremony), to not get married. Perhaps as the executive of the company you knew years ago that the company was not a good idea. These feelings or knowings are communications of what you should be doing, and if you decide to ignore these communications from Spirit then these communications or messages become louder and larger.

The Spirit is shifting you to become closer to its Source. When deeply awakened, you listen and hear the message and move ahead out of the relationship or company. You shift right away! This is called *visceral!* A deep inner knowing that you truly will follow, without question. You feel so deeply that you have no choice but to follow the message or communication. This could include decisions of not only relationships or job but moving from one moment to the next during the whole day – it is a flowing feeling. There is freedom in the flowing and a great comfort within the peace*full* flowing. It is within this flowing that *you live life!*

When in this space of living, you become so clear about everything that the universe then says, "Here is some more clarity, peace, flowing, freedom, love, stillness – all for you." Because you are attracting this. The universe has no choice but to move more of this in your direction.

This continues to relate and to parallel nature! Remember the tiny flower or grass poking out of the pavement crack has a smile on its face. It knows that it is growing up toward Father Sky and it knows that no matter what, nothing is stopping its growth. It knows that its seed will germinate and become a sprout. It knows that it will become a flower or grass stem. It knows that no matter what, all is fine. Its decisions are already made and in a blink of a sprouts eye it does not waiver its trust. It knows it will grow up between tough, cold, hard pavement. It knows it will see the sun. Even if it is stepped upon by a human foot it will return to the sun and the belly of the Mother.

As an awakened being, you as a Spirit in human form know you are Spirit and you know you are now living in this way of existing as one who is a container for Spirit as all of nature. Your task is to be the flower, be the stem of grass – just *be* – just flow and know! All of what you are creating in your life is coming from you. When in the awakened state of being you then create flow, freedom, love, passion, compassion, stillness, peace, and more because this is who you are! But you need to awaken, to turn on the light of who you are. When turned on, you then flow. In fact, once you turn on your light you realize the light is already on or All Ready on! You then get it! And everything changes! Because you change.

The Crystal Collectives within the All Truths state that when awakened or in a realized state, you begin to make connections quickly. In other words, you begin to acquire inner knowings that go beyond where you are able to go as a human being. Your awakened state allows you to make all connections. These connections are the connections that you would create when seeking your own decisions of life as well as connections within the outer world of yourself – connections to worldly issues, ideas, thoughts, feelings, and opinions being stated by the social media. Connections are made almost immediately as well as you begin to recognize synchronicities, which in fact occur not just once in a while or once a month but moment by moment. Synchronicities are then recognized and connected from one moment to the next. One second to the next second. You, as the awakened being, make all connections! What an exciting state of being – a state of ...

Awakened to all connections not only
within your inner self, but also
awakened to all that connects external of self and
awakened to the synchronicities of every second of the day.

Thus you ride throughout the day as if you were placed upon a glorious large white horse with no saddle or reigns because it knows exactly where to go. It takes you over the mountain and through the river. Or on the crooked path or the smooth bed of sand beside the ocean. Just sit and ride comfortably throughout the day – this day! Just try it and just feel this feeling. Just feel this knowing – that is all!

Healing – Wellness – Releasing

The next All Truth has scribed "healing, wellness, and releasing" upon a Crystal Collective and is saying that post-2012 the words *healing, wellness* and *releasing* will have completely different meanings and feelings. This means, due to the high vibrational energy frequency of people being awakened, that this is shifting the planet's vibration to a higher frequency. It is here within this higher frequency where you will discover that healing or recovery, releasing, and wellness of self move and shift very quickly. In other words, when the planet's frequency vibration of energy is low in vibration matching fear, anger, worry, and anxiety, then the event of recovery or healing, wellness of self, and releasing occurs very slowly due to the sluggish vibrations that it resonates. However, the higher the frequency the better and the more you are connected to Spirit.

When awakened to the realization that you are indeed Spirit, you then resonate a high frequency vibration. This vibration is then placed within the origins of the planet or its energy Spirit and then creates a higher vibration for the planet. When this vibration occurs for the planet, then the wellness of people changes to a higher vibration.

To explain further what the All Truth is saying requires the following: "when this time arrives, life will be filled with the Essence of a blooming flower as it gently unfolds one petal at a time." There are really no words to describe when this occurs, only a feeling – that is love and grace. An elegance of grace that will override fear, worry, and anxiety. The higher vibration energies clearly will increase the surrounding lower vibrations – this is an All Truth. This world of origin is a most magical place of health, releasing, healing, or recovery in an instant – this sounds almost unreal. Many people who are living fear based will believe this to be surreal and absolutely impossible. But why not try to believe this and see what happens instead of believing the opposite? Perhaps being an optimist would be handy for you. Perhaps being One in light, love, happiness, and grace would work for you.

The Crystal Collectives are saying that this way of being within the health field will occur and it can't help but not. It actually has no choice because of how the energy is laid out. The more people who become awakened, the higher the planet's energy vibration will rise.

This is truth.

Light from Father Sky

Light from the sun and light refracted upon the moon will begin to feel and look differently from now on. It will resonate a very different warmth and will feel softer and gentler and not so harsh. The light will not only feel softer, but will look differently. The intensity will not be so intense as it is now! This will shift only when people begin to awaken to the Spirit. In other words, the vibration of the earth will increase when humans become awakened and therefore this vibration will change the light from the sun and its intensity, color, and shape of light rays. As well, the moon and star lights will shift and change according to the higher vibration of the universe. When this occurs, the sun will also be less harsh in its energy as well as the stars.

Overall, what is being said here is that the higher vibration of the planet causes a softening. The harshness of everything begins to dwindle. As stated within the Crystal Collectives All Truth, "softening of everything will occur." This is a fact—nothing more and nothing less. This softening is the result of the higher vibration but also Spirit placing itself in a recognized state of being so that all can see and be amazed. The Spirit exposes itself and so does the sun and the moon! Now it's your turn to see the exposure.

More Bliss!

U pon further delving into the catacombs of the All Truths within the Crystal Collectives, it is important to remember that when you become awakened you may feel yourself become somewhat ungrounded. This is because of the *awesome amount of amazing realizations* occurring within you. This then means experiencing bliss, so much so that you are unable to connect with the realities of eating, sleeping, cleaning, and even working. You may begin this new awakened state in a feeling of being completely overwhelmed. This feeling of exuberance is natural for all humans who have come to new realizations of being awakened. Do not worry or fear this feeling for it is just a stage of awakening – it is that point of no return or that still point of realizing what is really going on here. When you begin to live in this still point, you may actually discover that life is and can be so different. You may even feel a little crazy because what you will learn and what you know may seem so surreal. Some humans have actually sat and stared into the sky in an ungrounded state of being for many hours. This is just you connecting to awe of Spirit or White Light. It means that you can stay in this way of living except that you need to eat, sleep, work, and tend to your needs and those of others.

You may decide to become a bit more grounded. To do this, you may wish to perform a meditation while sitting on Mother Earth. While in a quiet state with eyes closed, slowly visualize Mother Earth moving through your entire form from the bottom of your feet to the top of your head, soaking her completely into all parts of yourself and feeling her warm red energy soothing you back into the earthen rock. Stay in this visual until you are feeling completely grounded and planted on the Earth. This doesn't mean you have unawakened yourself; it just means you can function in life and the balance in life will come back. You may live or exist in this state for a little while. Just remember to sleep, eat, and rest properly in order for relaxation and contemplation to occur so that you may participate in the now – the present.

Sometimes when humans are awakened they are then downloaded with messages and realizations. If you are downloaded with messages and feelings, just relax, breathe and know that all is great for you now! Perhaps write these down or maybe this is a great time for you to open up your creative self. Those who have been awakened sometimes discover that creative ideas, visuals, songs, poetry, and writings begin to flow through them, sometimes immediately and sometimes in time – or in flow. If this does occur, pay attention to these and allow them to flow through you easily and fluidly. They are just birthing through you because you are a vessel for birthing that which is of peace, joy, passion, love, and compassion. Many creative humans have created art works, dance, music, rhythm, and writings of higher vibrational qualities when first awakened. This then proceeds into creating more as they become more connected to who they are – their awakened state of being.

When awakened, the creative door for each person automatically opens and blockages dissolve. Relax and unwind into this knowing as well because you may also become flooded with new and creative ideas. Just create and move fluidly one step at a time – slowly yet firmly planted or grounded. These are exciting times for all people. These times are the times for all to rejuvenate or rebirth!

Well-Being

This next Crystal Collective All Truth is named "well-being." The Spirit, when recognized, felt, believed, known, and allowed, will in fact become realized that it (the form) is filled with wellness, healthiness, and wholeness. This is what occurs when one becomes realized. People realize that their state of being is completely within the White Light of Source or Spirit. It is here within this knowingness, this believing, and allowing whereby a full, whole, healthy body reigns. It is within this way of being, one recognizes that the body is always well and in good order!

It is within the ego and the mind where the unwell and unhealthiness is created. What humans will begin to realize is that, as they open themselves up to the notion, the belief, and the realization that when living in an awakened state, they are capable of living an absolutely healthy and well lifestyle. It is here within the awakening where everything exists for you and all people. Health, wellness, and surety in abundance, compassion, and passion for all that you do, living a life filled with the soul's purpose of love. Everything becomes clear when you engage and immerse yourself in the state of awakening. You begin to realize that within the awakened state it is more than just a spiritual awakening; it is an awakening that not only awakens the Spirit but, wrapped within and around the Spirit, is the body. Therefore the awakening then acknowledges the body differently because you now have come to realize that the body is whole as well!

It begins with spiritual awakening. In other words, when you realize you are Spirit or you are awakened, you then treat your body differently. You begin to eat differently and realize in a deeper fashion that, yes, you are Spirit placed in a human form and this form is your "Instrument of Peace." This concept is beautifully captured in the song entitled "Instrument of Peace." It was inspired by the poetic words of St. Francis of Assisi and sung by Amy Sky and Marc Jordan.

> "Where there is hatred, let me bring love …
> Where there is silence, let me sing praise …
> For when we give love we will receive …
> Make me an Instrument of Peace …"

(Moccio, Stephan. *Instrument of Peace*, performed by Amy Sky and Marc Jordan. Latte Music/Mjay Music/Sony Music Publishing/Sing Little Penguins. 2006.)

The core of the form is the Essence where all things resonate from – it is pervasive. When one taps into the pervasiveness of this, the Essence then taps into a whole new way of being – of living. Your diet changes, you exercise more, you begin to feel a strong need to connect with nature. You begin to see, feel, taste, touch, everything very differently and with a gentle stillness. You then resonate at a high vibrational frequency and within this frequency you discover a freedom.

Those humans who are awakened feel free and alive in life so much so they even look younger – without any Botox or cosmetic operations. It is here within the energy vibration and the vitality of this energy, a younger appearance presents itself. This is common and for some people exciting. No matter, the ego loves the fact that you will look younger, so be careful because the ego is never satisfied. For example, the ego may state, "I don't really look all that young so I must not be completely awakened." Isn't this an interesting statement? Pay attention to the ego as you move through your life in the awakened state.

This All Truth is simply stating, "You are always healthy and well because you are Spirit, and do not allow the ego to change this thought, which is exactly what it wants to do. Be One within the Oneness of the universe."

4. Placing yourself in a state of completeness of soul and self-realizing. There is more to life than technology and information and reciting this information for all to learn because the ego quite enjoys this!

5. Placing yourself on the back porch and actually watching, feeling, smelling, and touching an approaching thunderstorm. Look how beautiful the rain is, hear the thunder, and watch the power of the lightening!

6. Placing yourself along the ocean's edge of sand and simply just lie there … listening to the breaking of the waves, touching the tender white sand grains, tasting the salty ocean, feeling the warmth of the sun upon your face, and then in the evening viewing and feeling the amazement of the glorious shimmering sunset.

The Crystal Collective within this technology scroll is stating search *nature, simplicity, stillness,* and *love.* That is all! Nothing more. Technology, of course, also includes medical technologies, transportation technologies, corporate technologies, protection for/of the country technologies, and so on and so forth. The Crystal Collective is stating all technologies will slowly dwindle away between now and the immediate future. As the origins of the planet approaches and more people are being awakened, then the energy vibration increases thus resulting in an energy increase vibration on the planet. When this occurs, more people will become awakened because they are seeing others change, hearing more about Spirit, and more.

Have you ever noticed people who use technology or have invented technology have a hard energy edge to them. This is in no way attempting to or being mean; it is just simply stating a fact. People who do not use technology or are very limited in their usage have a softer energy vibration. This is because of the energy or the electromagnetic field exuding from the electronic equipment – this energy enters the person causing a harsher edge to their energy field.

As one loosens one's hold on technology, he/she moves toward a fuller state of existing in One with Spirit. The Crystal Collectives by no means are stating that tech people are of very low vibration – it is stating that there is an energetic impact from the high usage and experimentation with technology. Therefore move yourself as far away as possible from technology as this is the post-2012 way of living. And instead implement the following spiritual technology:

1. Wireless-free connection to Spirit (no dial-up waiting).
2. Delete anything in your life that is placing you in a suffering position.
3. Shift keys to capitalize *Spirit* and *Oneness*.
4. Return to self, which is Spirit.
5. Power off to ego. Power on to Spirit.
6. Refresh, refresh, refresh, meaning rejuvenate back to nature.

Just try it!

Stillness Is Your Core

Within your stillness of self is your energy stream of life – it is your way of living. It is a place you live and live forever – because stillness is the Essence of the unmanifested. It is the core of your being. It is within this core of existence the *now* performs its duties. The following duties of living in the now are scribed by this All Truth gracefully in the Crystal Collectives:

1. Pay attention.
2. Listen, feel, taste, smell, and touch everything.
3. Be present with your Spirit or the stillness of the now. This isn't just sensing everything with your senses, it is actually feeling the stillness – your isness, your soul being. Just being and nothing more than this.
4. When sitting in the forest, feel the energy(ies) of the nature Spirits around you. Feel their Essence because their Essence is in fact yours as well. When stationed within the sitting position in the forest and you are feeling the Essence of nature around you, you are feeling your now! Absorb this feeling and watch how the time really doesn't exist much because the stillness within you defines just that – stillness and nothing more – because there is no time. Time is an illusion when living in the stillness of now.

5. Feel the next now; feel the fluidity of Spirit and the emotions connected to it; feel the arrangement of the next now. The arrangement is just the next now! Every now or present moment has one to follow – if it wishes and if it is in the best spiritual path from Source.

6. Finally, *just be*. Don't think about anything – just be in the feeling. Some would call this meditation. Isn't it funny how we need to shift into meditation in order to feel the present moment or the now? Just imagine what life would be like if every second of the day was living within a meditated state of stillness. Yes, of course you would be grounded because when in stillness, you are already immediately grounded. You are still and nothing more than this! You are not reacting to anything; you are responding to everything. You are not emotionally here or there but solid in emotional form. When ungrounded, you become emotionally strained with forms of emotional ups and downs. It is within the stillness whereby everything is created, decided, discussed, and implemented. In other words, this book of channeled works is birthed from a gentle stillness with no emotional attachments. Art work is birthed through the gentleness of stillness. Everything resonates from stillness. Being still is the key and nothing more.

Live out of time because being in the now has no time. Time is irrelevant. Now is the only time … nothing more. Why then is this book about the future into 2012 and then 2013, 2026, and beyond written? Isn't this a future discussion rather than a now discussion? Yes, this is correct on one level, but, on a feeling and spiritual level rather than an intellectual level, now is always Spirit. When one exists through Spirit or Spirit exists through One, then the now reigns onward on a linear line that is straight and never ending. It is the line of now. Imagine it to be just a silver white line that is alive in Spirit and all it does is stay steadfast in the time of now. This line of now is the stream of the highest Christ consciousness of the All Truths within the Crystal Collective. It is Source! This line is the line of being! It is here already!

By living now in every moment you are then creating every other moment after this moment through the energy of your emotions, thoughts, ideas, and opinions. Thus streaming into the law of attraction, which says, "I will give you more of these now moments *to live.*" Accept these beautiful still-filled moments from now until eternity. This silver white line is eternity – an eternity of nows. Within this eternity of the now line is the Crystal Collectives of energized messages scribed spiritually for those who are awakened to live by, which, if you awaken or are awakened, you already know what they are because you have been living in the now plane of existence.

The Crystal Collective messages are messages scribed in the out of time being now. For example, when you experience the point of the awakening in a now moment, you then have experienced everything now and forward, which is why one can become overwhelmed with not only emotion but with messages of what lies ahead on the silver white linear path of now. This is why it is scribed in the Crystal Collectives that one must rest, sleep, and eat properly because one will need to slowly digest the emotions of bliss, love, peace, passion, and compassion and the messages following or intertwining with it. This is most important information.

This book then is in channeled form retrieving the now messages in printed form in order to feel, see, and sense the possible now's from this now, which remains out of time. In other words, the now linear line is one of several now's strung together to create a most amazing eternity of Spirit and original world – origin within Spirit.

Accept in Love

This next Crystal Collective will assist in determining how you feel about what life has to offer you. It depends if you live from fear or love. The All Truth states, "If you reside in fear, then you block everything that needs to come forward. If you reside within love, you then reside with openness and a way of being One with all that can arrive for and to you."

When open in love, you are open to receive everything and all it takes is faith to surround yourself in order to accept all that you can receive – this is called *abundance*, which is all inclusive. When you are awakened to this state of realization, you then engage in a situation where all things and all spiritual domains and dimensions of emotions, ideas, and thoughts will arrive for you. This abundance then knocks on your door. All you have to do is open this door to your heart. The door needs to open in order to allow all that you wish to allow in, *great-fully*. This is called awakened and this is the state where all possibilities open and thus the original world appears and evolves to a new way of existing. What this means is the following:

1. When awakened, you may decide to switch or change your job situation or you change within your job situation.
2. You see, feel, hear, taste, touch, or sense everything differently. In fact, all of your *chakras* open up

and are ready to engage in a new way of existing. When this occurs, you begin then to realize that your ear chakras begin to open up, meaning you then hear Spirit at a much more intense frequency. Your third eye chakra opens, which is in the middle of your forehead above your physical eyes. When this occurs, you are then able to see White Light Spirits of love. What this then also means is that you become more aware and open to your opening of your five senses, and all of your chakras and the newly formed chakras. These new chakras are around your energy field and within your energy field. They are being created in order to assist in the thinning of the veil that is your body.

3.   You begin to feel differently. You feel as if you need to spend a lot of time being inner – going within and just feeling who you are. This time alone is most needed when you feel that you want to just rest and listen to Spirit. What you will begin to realize is that the more you look inside, the more realized you become to the awakened state and then the more you will be able to integrate this quiet inner way of being externally to others, work, family, friends – deeper realizations begin to occur as you go deeper!

4.   You may also begin to think within more spiritually bound thoughts that align with Spirit. When this occurs, all of life changes before your eyes. You notice things differently and you are attracting that which you are reflecting back to the universe. It is here within this reflection where you begin to realize that what you think and feel you attract to yourself.

5. New creative endeavors or even adventures may occur as you begin to realize that when you enter the stream or the flow of Spirit you then enter into a most amazing and creative way of being.

6. You may even re-evaluate your current employment situation, relationships, and purpose but also where you live and how you live. When you become awakened, you begin to seek places or living arrangements that match your spiritual existence. You may, for example, decide to unclutter, clean thoroughly, grow a vegetable garden, sell your home, and move to where you are drawn. These are common next steps that people take when awakened or realized. You begin to rest and realize that your exterior life now needs to shift, change, and align with your now way of living.

7. The All Truths within the Crystal Collectives message to you to speak your truth and nothing more than that. Just be who you are and live who you are.

Redesign of Community

This next Crystal Collective discusses the All Truth message about "the ways of religions or ceremonies." Some religions, churches, sects, tribes of people, and more will need to be recreated and felt differently. Between now and post-2012 people will become more attuned or awakened to what Spirit really is and then their ways of worshipping change. Certain religions, tribal activities of certain peoples, shamanic ceremonies, and others will all change their focus, ideas, theories, philosophies, dance, and music to a different form that will resonate at a higher vibration than what is presently occurring. And worship will become celebration.

This, as you can see, coordinates with everything else that has been stated through the messages of the other Crystal Collectives. Just simply observe. You will see churches begin to either change their way of worship or some may even close their doors because more people are becoming awakened to who they are and wish to connect and form community at a very different level – a deep spiritually filled level, thus the creation of communities and support gatherings. This is in no way indicating that all forms of churches or religious ceremonies are not of White Light, but they will be just simply transitioning into a different form of celebrating.

During 2012 and then post-2012, you, as a human, living at this time will experience some of the most profound changes in the world. Changes can sometimes be difficult for humans, however when the word *change* is replaced with the word *awakened* then the changes or the transitionings are much more in tune with peace or a smoothness. It will be like slowly moving from one room to the next room in a comfy old house. The changes or transitions will be ones of ease and clarity of mind, body, soul, Spirit, and emotion. Within the transitioning there will be several awakenings or as some people say *ah-ha* moments. One then moves forward within this ah-ha moment or point. This term *point* has been used several times throughout this book and is most important because at the points of the emotion of awakenings, this is when the transitioning will occur. Awakening is a feeling and not an intellectual activity. It is within the feeling whereby everything is created or manifested, not the intellectual capabilities.

This returns us back to "flowing in life through Spirit and emotion," then interject your intellect to amalgamate all of your insights. The emotional flow occurs first and the intellect follows – that is all!

Transitioning is occurring and so do not be fearful, worried, angry, filled with angst because the stream of the power of the Spirit will inevitably lead the way for you – that is it! Yes, for some this may sound very Pollyanna-ish, but it is not. Remember too that Pollyanna was a young child who changed the energy of a village because of her beauty, joy, grace, and love.

Some humans will choose to not awaken or be realized and this then becomes their life. They will see, feel, and sense that others have changed, however they and the ego's influence may decide not to see or feel the awakening within them. And this is okay because perhaps they need to see and feel more around them first. Other people are role models and extremely important for them to witness in order to freely engage in this shift to the original world. What this means is that as more spiritually evolved events occur in the world, they then will begin to see, hear, and feel reason.

It has come to a point where people have to make the choice of how to live. It is here within these decisions where the point of realization of the revelation of being awakened occurs. Within this point of feeling, life changes and then transitions. The revelation is the returning to the point of Spirit. Do not worry or be afraid for those who have not been awakened. All is in perfect timing for all beings.

Tiny Crystal Messages

This next Crystal Collective is one that includes several separate little crystals of messages as enveloped by the All Truths. These tiny crystals of messages are those that arise out of the bottoms of the large crystals. These smaller crystals have been placed in these spaces and are waiting for that perfect time to be revealed and are being prepared for the revelations.

The revelations within these tiny crystals indicate the fact that all beings are gathered as One and are not separate. These tiny crystals are the adjoining crystals that are used for the glue or the solid energetic connection between one being and the next. Have you ever noticed that once you become awakened you almost immediately find someone else who has also been awakened? When this occurs, you are joined to each other through and by these tiny crystals that become activated. This activation is the energetic release of the message of peacefulness, joining in Spirit, rejuvenation, and honoring self and others. Thus the reconstitution of all of life begins with you who builds to include others and thus the tiny crystals become activated by and through you.

These tiny crystals can then be activated with connections to and from anybody who is aware of awakening or is awakened or is becoming awakened. Because just this slight awareness that you are Spirit in human form activates these crystals of joining and thus you feel something occurring. Then they are revealed just at this perfect time, which you have defined through your realization that you are Spirit first and foremost.

Also know that these crystals can and may be activated even as you just walk through nature because nature too has availability to these tiny crystals. Once you begin to feel connected to Mother Earth/Father Sky, these tiny crystals will bond with you. Do you see how this works? Each as a partner – each working together as One – thus once again the Oneness of the Spirit/White Light/Source.

The Cycle of Life

These Crystal Collective All Truths are indicating to you that "the cycle of life" will shift dramatically because, as the original way of being approaches, you will see that the cycle of life is no longer a cycle but an immeasureable line. A line that is streamed directly from Source. What this inevitably means is that this cycle of life is no longer about life and death or time but about the shifting and the shifts of life. This means you will discover that your form or your veil is slowly transitioning into a formless existence or transparent existence; this is not death but transitioning.

If you are living in these times or days right now, your form or body is thinning and if you so choose to come back or reincarnate into another human form in your next life time then you will notice that your form will even be thinner or the veil will be thinner. The spiritual existing part of you will shine even brighter through you. As the Homo-Luminous form draws near, you will notice that more people will experience a stronger connection to Spirit as the veil thins, which is, as stated, the body.

Death will no longer be recognized as death but life shifting and changing because as the veil thins you have more access to those who have crossed over. There will come a time and it has already started – this time – of channeling, seeing, hearing, feeling, and touching those friends and/or family members who have crossed over. You can actually communicate with them now today and this will increase even more as the veil thins and more people will have access to communicate with those who have crossed over.

Death will no longer be. The cycle of life will no longer exist as a cycle but as a straight line following the Crystal Collectives stream of messages as well as following the spiritual evolution of all that is of love and shifting closer to Source. How does this translate to plant, animal, sea life, birds, and their cycle of life? The plant, animal, and sea life kingdoms are *already* there. They are already within the grasps of the Homo-Luminous form. They are already within this way of being, this form of existence. They are the direct and absolute direct connection to love and Source/God/White Light.

Their cycle of life is again lying upon a crystallized line or alignment to Source/God/White Light. What this means is within the death of beings, plant, animal, and sea kingdoms, is the absorption into Source. The difference here is that the plant, animal, and sea kingdoms already know they are Source/God and already know they are White Light and they already know all! They already are awakened to their existence as a Homo-Luminous being. They are aware of the flow in and of life. They don't need or require any form of still point of awakening to any state of realizations. Thus they are already there!

All become One in self within the plant, animal, and sea kingdoms. The decaying of a plant quickly and restoratively creates another plant. Immediate results are seen from an energetic and spiritual position because the tiny Crystal Collectives within a plant are opened always and filled with messages about not only life about the plant but about life as a whole. When this plant finishes its life, the Crystal Collectives within it re-enters the belly of Mother Earth and it sends messages to the Earth to say, "Here I am. Here is my life force. Take my tiny Crystal Collectives and grow another plant. I give to you myself not only alive in form but in its decayed position as place." Its energetic Crystal Collectives are therefore the energy/Spirit of who these plants really are. They are living the way of the Homo-Luminous form of existing. This form of existing is a form that is transparent. It is here within this form of existing where you will become filled with all that is of peace, joy, love, bliss, and more.

The human should learn from this kingdom what life is like living within the Homo-Luminous form. Just be One with God/Source/White Light. Flowing throughout the day one millisecond by one millisecond, for the entire day. For example, a leaf in the fall season does not question whether or not it should turn red or orange – it just happens and it just occurs because it is flowing with Source. It is flowing with all that is of love!

Learn from this kingdom who you are. You are this kingdom as well, but humans continue to believe in the ego of suffering. This is what makes them a material form and even thicker than the planet, animal, and sea life kingdoms. Humans are of a different form because they have a belief in ego. So when the ego is dropped or released, then they begin to return to a Homo-Luminous state of being. They are transparent and they are *Spirit aware*. How can a tree not be a Homo-Luminous? It has a Spirit; it communicates; it is God/Source; it is One! Since the human is more complex than the plant, animal, and sea life kingdoms, it is spiritually evolving in a more complex manner. Humans need to learn from Nature, from the belly of Mother Earth and Father Sky.

Higher Self = Knowing

This next Crystal Collective All Truth has energetically placed in this scribed scroll a message concerning "Higher Self." Within the crystals of Higher Self, the following is being revealed, shared, and, for some, confirmed.

The Higher Self is the self that is Spirit. When one says, "Connect to your Higher Self," what that person is actually saying is for you to connect or awaken to who you really are – Spirit in human form. Defined this means that when you are awakened to who you are – Spirit – then the Higher Self is allowed to lead your life through the flow of Spirit – that is all! The Higher Self is the self that is you – Spirit. You are connecting to Spirit. Also you can connect to other White Light Spirits, angels, archangels, and other White Light forms through the recognition of yourself as Spirit. Some humans are able to connect to the Spirits of nature and hear their messages, while others are able to talk to the belly of Mother Earth and receive her messages.

As you connect to your Spirit, which is the core Essence of who you are, you are then connecting to your Higher Self – your authentic being. This is the self that you need to listen to and follow and allow it to guide you throughout your days/hours/seconds.

The Higher Self is the only self that is Spirit. This is *who you are*. This Spirit is enfolded in the instrument or tool named body. Begin now – today – to use the body as if it were a musical instrument just by allowing the music to be played through you.

The music is Spirit and the body is the instrument. Life is like this and nothing more than this! You see when you allow the allowing to occur then the clarity of the tones, vibrations, and notes of song ring through you for not only yourself to enjoy but for others to embrace as well. You are an instrument of peace! You are an instrument of love!

The original world will be completely led by instruments of peace and love. It is now finally the time that humans grow up in Spirit and use this spiritual *device* as the new *vice* for life. This is truth, meaning freedom. You know the statement "The truth will set you free," which is exactly what is being discussed: the truth of living that life of love and peace. Both are Spirit; both are you! Both are your Higher Self. When one lives from this place, the law of attraction will say, "I will give you more of this …" The Spirit will give you more – more will be attracted into your life: that resonates with White Light and peace.

This Crystal Collective's All Truth of Higher Self states, "As you move through life from Spirit, you then also increase your energy's vibration. And as you increase your energy's vibration, you will then match the law of attraction and manifesting at *this* vibration of finer energies."

When living through your Higher Self, all that you wish for, feel passionate about, and more will manifest for and to you at that high vibrational level. It is within this vibrational level that you resonate and it will be *matched* by the Spirit or the law of attraction. Within this matching, one always needs to be aware then, where one's vibration level is resonating. By your vibration and through your vibration is the abundance or the manifesting stream. This stream is activated and will flow according to your vibration. It is within this stream all things are created. For example, receiving that phone call or meeting somebody at that perfect time, completing a project through unexplained timing, and so on. You see, this stream of Source consciousness begins to flow through your *trust* of the universe. This trust is simply trusting your Higher Self, your real and only way of being, which is through Spirit. Building this trust is really the only way to live and exist in the fullness of self. Trusting then is the key here and nothing more. Trusting means that you are trusting that everything is being fully worked and organized by Source – by the consciousness of Source. If you don't trust yourself, then you do not trust Source. The One that gave you breath. The One that created every part of you.

Within the trust, the Crystal Collectives indicates that if you have no trust then life becomes fully engaged in being and living away from Source because you are declaring Source to be not trustworthy! When this feeling of mistrusting of self and/ or others arises, then you will attract more of this into your life because of how the universe works. Eventually what can happen is you then confirm that Source can't be trusted because you are attracting more mistrusting events into your life. You see how this works? You must trust that when you begin and continue to live from Spirit you are saying to the stream of the consciousness of Source that you are prepared or preparing for what needs to occur in order to increase the vibration of not only yourself but the earth – this is what is being stated.

The Crystal Palace is fully organized energetically to reveal itself individually and to all people who have decided that this is their way of being from this day forward. Allow yourself to just release into this original way of being and trust the Spirit or Higher Self. This Higher Self is a term that was phrased by Spiritualists and Philosophers to denote that part of humans that is love, life, peace, and so on. However, this term is no longer in the year 2012 and onward or past 2012 because this term just simply means Spirit. When one says, "I just listen to me," then the *me* means Spirit of self; there is no longer any need to use other terms. It is a knowing that you are tapping into. It is this knowing where you will become fully engulfed, meaning, as the Crystal Collective All Truths state, "the knowing is the Spirit of who you are – the allowing is the trust of the Spirit and believing is the fullness of the allowing to trust or know."

By knowing you are trusting. Knowing and trusting are felt by silence and stillness. When you know something for sure, there is stillness and peace. For example, you know that 1 + 1 = 2 and feel very confident that this is true and have allowed this belief to resonate through your entire life. What would occur and how would you feel if someone said 1 + 1 = 2 actually no longer holds true? You would 100 percent dispute his or her notion. A deep inner knowing is Spirit and it is living through this Spirit and nothing more. You know that 1 + 1 = 2. You know that you are Spirit because of this deep knowing and you also know that everything is perfect and that all is Spirit.

Everything is in perfect alignment, so how does it feel when you are unknowing? Perhaps you are believing and feeling that something is occurring in your life that is moving into the unknown. For example, you have decided to move into a different city, new job, new this, new that – you may feel and believe all this to be unknown! But if you move to this city with a knowing that you need to move to this particular city, then the unknown is no longer the case because the knowing or the peace of the knowing will take care of everything.

This strange and fear-based term *fear of the unknown* should no longer be used because it is implying and in fact encouraging fear, which is of course believing in something that hasn't even happened yet. Imagine this – wasting all this time fearing the unknown – so you get up in the morning and decide to become fearful of the unknown. Fear meaning *F*alse – *E*xpectations – *A*ppearing – *R*eal or *F*orgetting *E*verything is *A*ll *R*ight. What this implies is that you should then be afraid all the time, especially if you wander away from knowing, Spirit, and trust. This now sounds so trivial.

You see, within the knowing or the peace is the assuredness that all is perfect. Wrapped tightly around and through the unknown is the known. Even though I am unsure what the details of my life are or will be, I know for a fact that all is good and perfect. Thus Spirit takes hold of form and uses this vessel as an instrument of peace!

This Crystal Collective information is quite simple and you can see how new theories, philosophies, religious views, and more will change because the only important piece of the Crystal Collective is the term *knowing,* and it stems from Higher Self. The term knowing goes deep and resonates at a higher vibrational energy than Higher Self. It refers to a whole new level of connecting to Spirit.

Within the wisdom of these collectives of crystals remains the essential core belief system of knowing. This knowing is most powerful and poignant. With this knowing, all else changes, in fact everything changes. One needs this knowing in order to succeed in becoming awakened to the real you as Spirit. The knowing is followed by the receiving. In other words, when you know, then the receiving will occur followed by the accepting.

Knowing, receiving, and accepting are feelings most important when delving into the spiritual part of you! It remains vital that when you accept the knowing and receiving that you also give forth gratitude. Always give forth gratitude, always! What this means is that you are saying thank-you to you as Spirit and to the Source/God for its blessings and wonderment, thus accepting who you really are!

Relationships

his next Crystal Collective All Truth will address the issue of relationships. Relationships will also change because your new way of being will surely shift and remold your relationships with all people. This shifting or movement of your relation to relationships will focus upon your feelings stemming from your Essence.

This All Truth states, "When you live and exist from the place of Essence, all relationships will indeed shift and change for the better because you now feel different." This coincides with the way you live and exist, which means the awakened self now determines all pieces concerning you. You don't feel revengeful, you don't feel stuck in anger, you don't feel addicted to suffering and pain. These toxicities are now quickly revealed and transformed. You just no longer need these toxicities to function in relationships. Furthermore, you discover your patterns of behavior in relationships. Are they negative, abusive, degenerating by others and/or yourself? Or are they one of beauty, peace, and of high vibration? You then begin to loosen the hold of your patterns of negative relationships and releasing these patterns is of utmost importance. It is here within the releasing where new foundations for relationships are planted, sown, and harvested. It is in this newness of planted seeds and seedlings whereby everything occurs within your relationships.

During 2012 and post-2012 you will experience some very important shifts and movements within all of your relationships. This will occur to all beings as they become attuned to the shifting of the Earth – to the original world – the original state of being.

Isness

This Crystal Collective All Truth message deals with beingness, which means knowing where self already is, which is within the *isness* of self. It is *self.* It just *is.* You are this – the isness of being. You are the great tidings of grandeur, which means who you are by just being you. The All Truths are stating you have arrived just in time to be who you are – that is a being of love, peace, blissfulness, and passion. The passion is living your life through love. Your passion is that which you call yourself through your love of self and others – your "being-ness" – and nothing more.

Just be you – who you are! Just arrive gently into your way of existing in life – nothing more or less. This is one of the most powerful or power-filled messages from the Crystal Collectives.

Also "always realize that you are influencing others – do not feel that you are not influencing others." Do not feel that you are alone when awakened. The one who is living within oneself actually determines who you are. In other words, yes, sure be within yourself but also be external of yourself. Just be! Since you will and are always influencing others, whether you know it or not. It is just the way things are – just this! When you need to move within your interior this is okay. Rest there until you feel you can shift outside yourself. This shifting is most important because it is the realization that you are feeling the need to serve and help others. This feeling is the next layer of being awakened – that is all. It is the isness of you shining or blossoming forth and forward. So stay within until you are able to venture beyond the exterior of self. All is in perfect timing and order.

Golden Strings

Intertwined within all of the Crystal Collectives is the thread or the golden strings of Spirit, when defined means that these golden strings are strings of messages that attach to one Crystal Collective then another then another. These golden strings depict the solidity of stillness within the crystals. It is here where the continuous measure of love is strung and is passed from one Crystal Collective to the next along the line of peace or stillness.

Each message from each and every collective has a common golden string streaming through it, which is the *golden thread of stillness*. Within this golden thread is the energetic transportation or movement of stillness. These golden threads just carry stillness, peace, trust, faith, bliss, and joy from one Crystal Collective to the next. Therefore creating a uniformity of spiritual guidance for all.

Whenever you read or perhaps reread a Crystal Collective's All Truth message, feel the common feeling of peace that moves from one collective to the next collective. Feel the commonality(ies) of each of these and allow yourself to be touched by and through these threads of stillness. For this is truth and nothing more than truth. How beautiful this is and how wonderful this is to actually become One with the golden thread.

You are that golden thread! Which means you create the stillness of Spirit within yourself. You just simply awaken yourself and, when awakened, you then realize that you are that golden thread – that solidity of stillness, that peace-filled being. You are that! You are this being, a completeness of White Light – that golden thread of bliss.

Arise then to the occasion – the occasion of realization or being awakened. This awakened state is who you really are. This has been stated several times throughout this book and the repetition is meant in great purpose.

The golden thread is a thread that holds you. You are the peace. When you realize this, you begin to see, feel, touch, hear, and taste everything more clearly. Clarity begins to occur. You begin to realize that you are here on this planet for wonderful reasons, you are One with Spirit, you are peace, and you are the open vessel for Spirit to move through you.

So how can you not be that golden thread of stillness? How can you not be that movement of White Light? How can you not be that solidity of stillness? How can you not be awake in the ebb and flow of the tide of life? You are that golden thread because you are eternal and you are created by Source, therefore you must be part of Source – that insistent of peace. You are that instrument or that golden thread that connects every single Crystal Collective or All Truth. Without you, how would Spirit work on this planet?

You are the connectors. These connectors or groups of people are gathering more and creating a strength within each person and sending the gentleness of love, joy, peace, and bliss to all people. It is here within this love, joy, peace, and bliss where all people connect – thus the golden thread. This connector or thread is the Oneness of all people. When all people realize they are connected, they will become so aware of this Oneness that clarity of trust and having faith just simply bursts forth.

Arise to the belief and the truth that you are this golden thread, the Oneness with all people, the connectors to all beings. The stream of peace from one Crystal Collective to the next. You are One in beauty and peace! Trust and believe that this is so!

Time as Illusion

The All Truths have scribed within these catacombs of the crystals that "time is an illusion." Time was only created by the human form in order to place measure, judgment, thoughts, and opinions upon the planet Earth and all that entails the planet. This is the way that the planet Earth has been operating for centuries.

Time is just an illusion and when humans live through and by time they create that which is illusion. This illusion of time was created in order for everything to occur. Time was history – which is *now* – where all people need to begin to see through the lens of illusion. Time is just part of that illusion, which means that time is simply an empty void! A void that has no meaning – a void that has been exposed as one large space in time. It is a place in time where everything exists. Time just goes on and on. It has no beginning and no end. It just continues and maintains its way of being – nothing more than this!

The All Truth states that people are living within the grandest of times when they will believe, allow, and know that time is irrelevant. What does this really mean? It means that, as one moves through life, one's Spirit remains the same and it has no ending. Therefore there is no time attached to and within Spirit. However, realize that the human form has an expiration date on it and may be considered time from this perspective.

Furthermore, consider this question: If you removed worry, anxiety, confusion, frustration, fear, and anger from your day, wouldn't the time in the day expand and become larger in form? You would create hours within your day to just enjoy, rest, relax, serve, and receive? If you removed fears, worries, or anger, then time would increase dramatically. Even removing future or past thoughts would increase your time within the present.

Time is stuck within the psyche of the mind of humans. It is within their thoughts, beliefs, opinions, and judgments. If, for example, you hear, "You are late picking me up today," but within this presumed lateness some amazing events occurred for that person arriving to pick you up. These events were meant to occur; the person was meant to be late and you were meant to slow down. When flowing with emotion and Spirit you are never late, you just *flow* in perfect timing.

Everything is in perfect order and when one flows with intuitive emotions and Spirit then one creates a most beautiful place or point of being. Within this point of being there is an emptiness or a void that is the feeling of the illusion of time. It is here where you create life within the flow!

This original world is evolving out of the void and this void is opening and will open up completely to the idea that all beings will live from this place – a place of surety, of compassion, passion, love, and bliss. It is here within these emotions that life is felt. It is here within these places you are able to create your way of being. When flowing from the emotion from your Spirit, time then becomes irrelevant. You begin to feel a difference in everything that you do. You begin to know, believe, and feel that everything is perfectly planned just for you. You begin to believe, know, and allow all synchronicities to be revealed to you. It is here within these synchronicities and your recognition of these synchronicities where *time* becomes an illusion. Once you recognize this, then even further awakening occurs.

Awakening to the real time, which is a void. Therefore, you don't need to rush, you don't need to become frustrated that you are late because you encountered a most amazing story on your way to picking up somebody, and it gave them time to just be quiet. All is perfect!

Synchronicities happen one millisecond at a time, not just occasionally but one millisecond after another, and if you felt this as truth then life would be so much easier for you. You may begin to feel bliss! You may begin to understand differently what life really means. This is *the beginning of the end of time as we know it*. Perhaps you have heard this mystical statement before and now understand and feel what this means.

It is now time to end time! Don't, however, get this confused with arriving to work not on time or picking up a friend hours later than expected (unless an event/occurrence within the space happens) and with all due respect to self and others the balance of flowing with the balance of being grounded is vital. Both of these need to work hand in hand with the thinker mind in place. You feel your flow of Spirit and then respond to it through the balanced, grounded mind. You don't react. You gently respond. This original world or life will be filled with most exciting events and times.

Point of Feeling

The point whereby all decisions are made is based specifically upon a point within time. However, time is an illusion. So the point is the feeling and not an actual clock or scheduled time. It is the point at which you decide that you wish to be awakened to who you really are.

It is the point when you decide wholeheartedly that you need and require yourself to become immersed within the new way of being or the original state of being, meaning who you really are and what you are all about! You are all about your Essence, stillness, Spirit, and nothing more than this! This point of decision will then include questions, such as *How do I awaken? When do I awaken?* and *Do I need to take a course to learn how to awaken or read a book?*

The Crystal Collective messaged scribed from the All Truths is saying that you just need to "decide and then at this point in feeling, transitioning will occur." The transitioning is wrapped around the "point of feeling." The point of feeling needs to be genuine and a deep inner knowing (not wisdom but a knowing) will emerge and welcome you! At this point, Spirit evolves itself through you to a revelation of a realization that you are awakened. When at this point in feeling, further ideas, opinions, and more blossom forth from you into realities of how to now transition your life.

What does transitioning mean then? Transitioning ultimately means "shifting, moving, switching, and engaging."

Enlightened

This next Crystal Collective will encompass the following information as messaged within the All Truth of the universe. It will deal with all that represents the term *enlightenment* or *enlightened*.

When you awaken to the realization that you are an enlightened being, then your life will change and become so filled with love that you have no choice but to give and serve in a loving manner. This is a most beautiful and serene space for not only for yourself but for others as well.

Welcome this serenity when it occurs and give gratitude for receiving this knowing that you are enlightened and furthermore you are then able to shine out the Light of who you really are.

When awakened to the realization that you are an enlightened being, you then shift and become free in serving all and accepting or receiving all. When you accept this place of living, you then really begin to live. You also then begin to understand that, as the veil thins (the body), you become more accessible for the Spirit/Source to shine or move through you. You become filled with serving others and accepting all of the gifts that the universe offers. What you give is what you receive back from the universe.

When the veil thins, the body form thins and the Spirit/Source shines through you. Your eyes shine with Spirit from within and yet you are still grounded. This sense of groundedness is centered in self – in the knowing that all is in perfect order and believing that you are in a state of wonder and aliveness, even though you are within this form. You are living in a fashion that is of love, joy, bliss, peace, and stillness. As your veil or body form thins, you become attuned to the Oneness of self and the Spirit/God/Source. As you and many others shift your lives into the awakened state of realizing that you are already enlightened, you will relate to others who have also awakened to their enlightened being of self.

When living through Spirit, you will be grounded in Spirit and able to allow Spirit to work through you, and you will be able to also discern everything! In other words, when you discern, you also are able to make further connections in life. Also, through discernment you are able to connect back and through to your body. Allow all that is to occur for you and allow all that needs to be. Be who you are!

Manifesting

This Crystal Collective within the All Truths will deal with the concept of co-creation or creation through manifesting. The All Truths of manifesting declares that "one should indeed be able to manifest whatever one requires." However, what has occurred is humans are attempting to manifest all that they feel they need, desire, and want. The laws will manifest this, but they will manifest this according to your level of vibration. You may desire or wish to manifest a large home stemming from your greed (low vibration), but what happens is that more greed and ego are manifested. Another example: if you *long* or *desire* to manifest love and/or happiness, then because you are *longing* and *desiring* you manifest only these feelings of *longing* and *desiring*.

What, however, will now occur within the All Truths of manifesting is that, when one manifests, one will manifest that which matches his/her vibration.

The abundance for all is large and bountiful. The abundance for all is there to be had and be grateful for. The abundance is here for all beings living within the All Truths. This means that you understand that what you manifest matches your vibration. Create a life that resonates love, peace, and a gentle yet solid stillness. You create that life where you are always surrounded by the White Loving Light and all of life is thus encompassing of this Light. Within this Light you are One with no greed, selfishness, or separateness from others but Oneness with all.

You are completely aware of the way to manifest through this vibration and you do so with ease because you are matching the Spirit or the law of manifesting. As you manifest what will assist you in serving others then you will receive back to you and become that vessel for and of manifesting more of the awakening – more of the White Light. In other words, co-creating life with Light, bringing in the stillest of the still to *your self* and others.

If, however, you are believing in ego, greed, and judgment, then this will be manifested back to you. You then will continue to experience more of this. However, this law of manifesting is also declaring that the clearer your heart and the more connected you are to Spirit, then the more opportunities you have to manifest in a crystal-clear way because you see you are the manifestor especially when living or being in a state of awakening.

When you flow and feel Spirit within your daily life, you then become this flow – because you are the fluidity of the flow. You are it! This is who you are. When awakened and living as the Homo-Luminous being of high vibration, you are the flow of manifesting moment to moment and nothing more. There is nothing to even think about or discuss when manifesting or when living in this awakened state because your feelings are the driving force to maintaining what is required in your life to serve.

If you decide to be awakened to this state and decide to always live from this place, then you will know exactly what these above words mean to you. You will know exactly what is being discussed. It really is just a feeling.

If however, you decide to live a life of lower vibration, then you will attract more of this because you are existing within the energy of lower vibration and what this may inevitably mean is for you to attract and manifest more of the same. Individuals who have awakened are able to realize and feel what this entails and the ways of manifesting from the ego perspective and the awakened perspective. This means that when awakened to stillness, these people are now able to compare and feel the difference between the two and know which way of being is of utmost importance. It is just a feeling.

Furthermore to this point of information is that if one has blockages within oneself, these blockages will then create blockages for manifesting, which of course coincides with everything that was just stated. If you are ego-based, one of selfishness, and greed, then this blockage will self-create the same. In other words, if one is living from the point of ego then this blockage within oneself will create more blockages.

However if you are unblocked, peace-filled, still, and in love with self and others, this creates an openness of energy or Spirit to enter fully to express co-creation.

Do not judge those who live under the illusion of ego as being filled with darkness and hopelessness. All they need to do is just taste the White Light and then they will want an elegant meal of gourmet food of White Light, not the heaviness of the ego.

Since we are on the topic of food, let us digress for a moment or two with another All Truth of food. Certain foods are considered high vibrational and low vibrational. High vibrational foods leave you feeling just that – high energy, light, and still. Low vibrational foods have the energies to leave you feeling, tired, heavy, slow, and low. High vibrational foods include organic fruits and vegetables, water, juices, organic grains, and so on – similar to a vegetarian way of eating. Low vibrational foods include sugar, dairy, gluten, starch (pasta and rice), meat, fish, and poultry. When living from a place of high vibration, one then *automatically* shifts into eating high vibrational foods. You see how this all flows together.

If you eat low vibrational foods, live an existence of heavy, negative thoughts, and allow ego to reign through you by bringing in suffering and confusion, you can determine how this would influence your life and what you manifest.

So now is the place for a new way of existing, a way of being One with Spirit that is within your form – you! Your God center or Source center.

Four Seasons and Weather

Accgording to this Crystal Collective All Truth, the newly formed Earth will experience weather seasons that are gentle and easy upon the human being. These new seasons of the original world will not be so harsh and so extreme. It is here within these seasons where you shall become filled with softness or gentleness. In the original world, you will no longer require such protective gear from the weather because the vibration of the planet will be such that you are engaged in the recognition that you are One with all beings because all are Spirit.

Presently perhaps one requires protection from the fierce and severe weather as experienced during these current times, but you will notice a slow calming effect that will begin once the energy vibration increases to a state of heart. This means more people are awakening through their hearts to discover that they are Spirit. As this occurs the Earth's vibration increases and the whole of the planet shifts its vibration and the seasons thus begin to change. This is also symbolic in meaning that little and eventually no protection will be required, meaning that, as one shifts and evolves into the Homo-Luminous transparent form, all protection will be unnecessary.

If you feel secure, safe, and protected, then you have entered an awakened state of being and are beginning to realize that when awakened you are engaged in being alive in Spirit. This means you no longer need or even require to place a protective barrier around yourself because you are White Light. You can set yourself free from all protections and protective garments. Fly freely into your life and through your life. Fly freely into the world of who you are. These protective garments are those that have kept you from living your full authentic self.

During 2012 and post-2012 you will see and hear more people shedding their protective coats of armor and being their authentic selves. It is within and throughout this self of freedom whereby you can *live life*. As people shed their protective gear, then others will watch and do the same. As this happens, the planet's vibration increases and the seasons begin to change. Yes, of course the material protective gear is still perhaps required due to the present extreme weather of hot and cold, but eventually the planet will soften its lines and itself to temperate weather and seasons. This is already beginning to occur.

Be free. Clear your protection, open up, soften your lines, ease your face, caress your heart, and open to who you really are – that is Spirit, soft and easy, One in freedom and bliss.

In Each Life There Is a Refrain

This Crystal Collective of an All Truth messaging is one that requests of you the importance of a song's refrain, meaning rest and verse of rhythm. "Each life there will be a refrain, a time of great change, a time of shifting, transitioning, moving into newness, a new beginning, a rebirth." *Allowing* is the key! This refrain for some may occur frequently and for others not so frequently. Each person has a certain time for his/her refrain – a certain designated space or gap. And what this means is that when one enters this space or place or gap of refrain, then this is where all decisions are made and created and life shifts and it could shift dramatically!

These refrains can sometimes occur when least expected yet expected; it is to say that one actually knows when these will occur within a deep level of knowing! Especially when awakened. You can feel it arriving. You can feel this gigantic shift coming in full abundance of joy, bliss, and glory. This is when all occurs for you! You are placed in yet another *still point* in life. Your first big spiritual still point was when you decided to choose peace, love, and bliss or therefore to be awakened. This next spiritual still point may be your calling – your absolute calling into life and what is required of you is to then choose: "Yes, I will go and live my calling" or "No, I am not ready yet." Thus the still point!

If this is occurring with you or you feel it arriving, just be still – be in a relaxed state and allow yourself to shift and move into a space that is of peace. Find this place and then make your choice. Your still points in life may occur during a refrain – a gap, a space, or a place of movement. It may be a phone call, a conversation, a poem you read, and more. Something in your life will cause a refrain. A song's rhythmic verse continues to sing throughout your life but the most important times may be the refrain – the resting point on the bar of notes, that still point of choice. What is going on? How am I feeling? You may even ask the questions *Who am I?* and *What is my calling?*

These refrains can happen anytime, but most occur when a person is between forty and sixty years old, during a midlife era when one is seeking within oneself and thus a refrain is created for him/her. It may begin by asking the above questions, and then the universe/Spirit says to you, "Okay, here's more of this, here's more for you to ponder and seek inside of yourself."

These refrains can be life changing! Be prepared in your awakened state in order to pull up love, peace, bliss, passion, and compassion. It is within this state whereby you are able to gently move into a great state of glory through this refrain. When experiencing this refrain, feel it completely. Feel it to its most wonderful grace. Be peace. Be love. And just refrain!

Medical Practice Changes

The message from the Crystal Collective within this All Truth states that "within the next number of years you will see medical practices change." The medical world will begin to take notice of people's emotional and spiritual status with great awareness. So much so that the medical world will more than ever partner with Naturopathic medicine, energy work, body talk, counselors of life, and more. A partnership will arise in the post-2012 era. This is because more people who work in the medical field will become awakened. When more medical professionals become awakened, then awakened medical influences can happen.

It also becomes helpful when indeed the patient has been awakened to his/her spiritual state and speaks to the medical profession as well. For example, if several awakened people said to the medical profession, "I will no longer take my medication because I believe and feel something different within me now," then the medical profession would need to pay attention.

In fact, post-2012 there will be a time when medication will be unused and it will be unusual to use it. There will be a time when birthing a child will be performed naturally and this will become a regular practice. There will come a time when people will declare themselves as purity of Spirit and soul and engage in living a life of grace, bliss, and love and then nothing will need to be healed.

Transitioning

This next All Truth discusses the precious message surrounding the "transition of life – or the transition into your new life/your metamorphosis." What this is indicating is that, as you shift into your new life of being awakened, many ideas and thoughts will emerge for you. You will be gifted with several blessings and miracles that will assist you on your journey or transition. It is here within the transitioning where the metamorphosis will occur. This process is the occurrence of you shifting fully into the Homo-Luminous body, which is clearly your awakened illuminated self that which is completely engaged in just living and being within this life of 2012 and post-2012. At this point in your life, you are resonating at a very high vibration and are serving your purpose or spreading love, peace, joy, and grace.

In order to transition to this next stage of metamorphosis, it is messaged from the Crystal Collective All Truth that you as the human simply "begin with one step at a time and engage in the process of shifting and transitioning to the metamorphosis stage." In other words, when a transition occurs, then within this transition you will discover the steps that will allow you to shift toward the next stage, which is the metamorphosis stage. These steps between transition and metamorphosis within the Crystal Collectives are those that are based solely/souly upon your decisions.

These are decisions where pieces of your life will make themselves known to you and you then decide if you wish to accept these or not. For example, when you have decided that being awakened is something you would like to experience and live, you then enter into the transitional stage where the awareness of what you wish to do and the transitioning of what you should do become co-operative with each other. They become a team with one another and this then leads to the metamorphosis. Within the transition stage you may realize that a decision to shift jobs, relationships or home may all need to change. These changes are all part and parcel with the movement toward the final metamorphosis or the illuminated body.

The crystals state that the transition between the *self of now* and the *self of illumination* is a most beautiful step because this is the process by which one must become engaged in order to arrive within the feeling of beauty, love, peace, joy, passion, and compassion or illumination. What this means is that through the steps between transitioning and the illumination metamorphosis, all signs, signals, and feelings of flow with Spirit need to be examined and noticed carefully from a spiritual perspective. This information is just simply stating that all steps within the process from transitioning to metamorphosis are yours and only yours.

It is within the awareness when full awakening or the illumination occurs. It is within this awareness of everything that is declared as presently now where the metamorphosis occurs. When you declare or state that you *get it* and finally see, hear, taste, touch, and feel *it* – then you are within the awareness – the awakened state which then slides into the Homo-Luminous state. These states are different yet very similar. In other words, when you have awakened to the awakening state, you then have allowed yourself and your Spirit to flow into the state of illumination, which means a state of absolute, complete, and fully engaged in being awakened. This final (if there is such a thing as final) stage of transitioning is then called the metamorphosis or the Homo-Lumination stage. This is the state by which the world we will live through and engage in is in the new Earth or the *original* earth, which is led vibrationally by and through these beings of the full Homo-Lumination or those who have been placed, through their own free will, into this state. This time on the planet will be post-2013 and the finalized or realized metamorphosis by about December 21, 2026. This date is most valuable because between now and then many world, personal, and community events, will occur in order to release all people into the final phase of 2012, which occurs during a perceived time of December 21, 2026. In other words, the All Truth is stating that not only are transitioning stages occurring within human beings but also within the planet, world, biospheres, atmospheres, and nature. All living creatures! This is occurring as each individual becomes awakened. Then this vibrational energy exudes and affects the world.

When transitioning, it is always best when dealing with large changes to ease into them in order for clarification to take place. When each individual recognizes who he/she is, then this will create the stages within the transition stage to shift to the metamorphosis stage. It is here within these different stages whereby you will become fully alive within your awakened state, thus creating a world as such – awakened and illuminated.

an energy. If, however, when you serve and you feel nothing coming back, then you need to accept the receiving. Perhaps the receiving is through the Spirit! Not from the human being. If the human has a blockage to serve or give, then receiving will also be blocked. It is an energy!

Many lessons are always learned through serving and receiving and accepting or allowing yourself to serve or gift then receive or vice versa. The holding hands of all people is in fact serving and receiving. Accepting, giving, allowing, serving, and receiving just through hanging onto hands. The holding of hands in a circle around the planet is the circle of life – the circle being the spiritual calendar or the Mayan calendar (as it is called) for original world. Complete and infinite! But for this to occur in a genuine fashion, community and connectors are a must! Community needs to occur! You see what is occurring here? The more the community comes together, the more the availability for the resonation of the higher vibration.

This is the meditation visual that all humans need to incorporate into their daily meditation practice. This is extremely important!

When awakened, you will know how important this meditation will be. You will realize and be awakened to the fact more will come into this planet to move people into gatherings and community. You may even begin to see community living shifting into a new way of being. In other words, some people may begin to move to a self-sufficient community or place of stay. These communities are already forming and being created now across the planet. Do not be surprised if you are drawn to this way of living. It is here with this way of living that one becomes filled with purpose, reason, love, and peace/stillness.

Revelations or a Revealing

The All Truths in this Crystal Collective entitled revelations states that "today is the greatest day for all beings because it is now a time for the revelation of the realized to occur." In other words, the revelations are the returning to origin. It is the removal of all in order to return! Return to the origin.

These are exciting, tranquil, serene times for all living beings. From now onward a *world of origin* is forming. The most interesting thing about all of this as stated in the All Truths is that "nature – Mother Earth – Father Sky already know about this." The plants, even the little wild violets that are so tiny, know what is going on! Humans are stepping up to the plate – this is a golden plate gifted by Spirit. This plate is of the new age or the origin. It has been cleaned, dusted, polished, and re-golded just for you to declare who you are, and that is Spirit in human form. These are indeed exciting, promising, and hopeful times.

The Spirits and the beings of nature know exactly what is going on here. The human beings are simply catching up – that is all! The message within every single Crystal Collective is "Nature knows." But as a human, you are also nature!

All of the plants, animals, sea life, birds, earth, and stars are awakened, no doubt. One star would never say to another star, "I so much want to be a brighter star like you!" A tiny, itsy-bitsy ladybug would never say to an eagle, "I so want to fly in the mountains and over the cliffs like you do!" A flower in seedling form would never say, "I so much want to become a purple flower, not an orange flower." You see, nature has no ego! Mother Earth and Father Sky have known forever about the shift and they too are making their origins be known very strongly and they speak to humans very forthrightly. They tell us the pollution is killing us, the water is lowering its level and quality, some of our animals and plants are becoming extinct, the birds are changing their songs, the whales are disappearing, the salt in the ocean is changing its mineral content, and so on and so forth.

Their communication to the humans has awakened some humans to the fact that all beings need to save the planet. The message is very clear and the communication continues and will continue until human beings awaken to who they as humans are – that is Spirit. When awakened, they then hear the planet! Why? Because they are more readily attuned and available because they get it. So here's what's happening! The Mother and the Father are speaking loudly and firmly, but they are also messaging information to people about the urgency and the need for the shift back to origin. They also know and feel that people are beginning to awaken and live their lives from this state thus increasing the energetic vibration of the planet, and a rejuvenation is just beginning to occur.

Next time you walk in the park, sit upon the belly of the Mother and gaze up to Father Sky and say loudly or softly, "I am here for you! I feel you. I am you." You see, as a human, you are One with the Mother and the Father. So when they shift, you shift. When you shift your energy, they shift their energy. All are One – that is it!

The Garden of Eden is the symbolized visual representation of the original world due to the fact that its representation is *the* origin! The Garden of Eden represents the feeling of the original world. The feeling of this place of utopia was one of love, peace, stillness, beauty, grace, passion, and compassion. Thus it was a place filled with Spirit and a purpose of love.

This visual or symbol of the Garden is exactly what nature is returning the planet to – the Garden of Eden, or another term would be Nature's Garden of Spirit where all things reside in peace, harmony, love, and grace. This place named Nature's Garden of Spirit is within each and every being. The ego is the temptation to mistrust, sabotage, and suffer, which is of course the "red apple." Symbolically it is an apple because the ego is always hungry for more suffering – it will never be full.

Nature's Garden of Spirit is within one's own self. When you awaken to who you really are, you then are able to tap into the Nature Garden of Spirit because you awaken that Natural Garden of Spirit filled with beauty within you. When awakened, this increases your energy's vibration, which then influences others around you energetically and also assists in the raising of the planet's vibration as well.

As one person then another becomes awakened and increases his/her vibration, then the possibility of another Garden of Eden or Nature's Garden of Spirit occurs. Not unlike the meditation of visualizing the planet Earth encircled by all humans holding hands to form a circle around the Earth and sending love, peace, stillness, and joy. These emotions of Spirit created the Garden of Eden and you too can recreate this beauty once more. It just begins with you!

The Crystal Collective's All Truth is indicating that nature knows the possibilities within the potential of the human. Mother Earth and Father Sky are depending upon *you* to help them out in recreating the most amazing Garden once again. This collective has been waiting for the perfect time to further expose its message. It is also saying that once beings are able to shift into the original world between now and post-2012, they will discover new forms of plants, animals, rocks and minerals, fish, stars, colors of sunrises and sunsets, soil, and so much more. *Everything* that is *every thing* in nature will and is just beginning now to evolve spiritually; as the human evolves spiritually, so does Nature. In other words, there will be discovered more healing plants used as natural remedies, a new species of fish will reveal itself that is a cleansing and calming energy for the ocean, new kinds of fruits and vegetables will be discovered that are extremely high in minerals and vitamins, new forms of stars exposed that cause brightness and glory in the night skies and even the colors of the sunsets and the sunrises will be changing.

When humans evolve spiritually, Mother Earth and Father Sky are also spiritually evolving – each matches each other and so on. This is a very exciting and gentle yet strong time for Spirit. It is a time when all of nature, including human beings, spiritually evolve, and as this happens the evolution becomes the revelations or the returning to the origin of life or the original world.

Conscious Way of Being

Become aware of any philosophy of the mind and form. The discovery of the id, ego, superego, subconscious, and more are no longer valid as far as understanding the consciousness of being. These concepts were created with a human perspective and are limited as to how they can explain *being*. Study, research, and discussion will no longer be needed in order to understand our being. It is within the catacombs of the Crystal Collectives where all of this information about being conscious and consciously aware is held.

Now there is only conscious awakening to who you really are and this is coming from within. Coming from the crystals within your form. Nothing else needs to occur. The information shared at this point in history was important because it brought us to the place where the planet is now.

The ego is being exposed, dismantled or kept in check as stated in several previous sections. Ego is no longer a valid term or concept.

These philosophies that create mental concepts of self or being are no longer holding water because the flood gate has opened and now is the time to receive the water of the new freshness of Spirit. Now is the time to be flooded with the fresh warmth of Spirit because this is who you are – Spirit. Now is the moment in time to awaken!

Rest and Awake

This Crystal Collective within the All Truths is one of "rest and being awake in life." What is being explained is the fact that these two states of sleeping and not sleeping will be strongly separate yet strongly together. In other words, when you are sleeping during the evening hours you will always be placed within a deep and wonderful REM sleep and when awake throughout the daytime you will be placed within a very awakened alive state. "Therefore when awakened, you will also become aware of sleep!"

Yes, even your sleep patterns will change. This of course makes sense since you are living from an awakened state and you have moved into a peace-filled state of being. This means you have not only raised your energetic vibration but as well, you are completely free of worries, anxieties, and fear and have shifted into a life of simplicities, relaxations, and meditations. When living from this point of stillness you then, of course, sleep very well, and in fact when within your deep state of sleep you may be transported into the astral – into the Spirit of purity. For many people, this is occurring already and perhaps they have not realized it. Perhaps you recall experiencing some wonderful White Light dreams that are intensely beautiful and filled with the notion of love. These dreams are you reconnecting to Spirit.

When living the awakened state, you will experience intensely beautiful and refreshing sleep and in fact you may not need as much sleep because you are placed in such a deep sleep state of being that is worry and anxiety free. This means you may need only a few hours of very deep REM sleep. This is extremely common for those people who resonate at a higher energetic vibration. Therefore the high vibrational energies are such that they place you into a sleep state immediately. For example, have you ever walked into an extremely high vibrational building or structure at night and felt the urge to immediately fall asleep? At a certain energetic point of evening (sunset) vibrations change in order to place humans in a calm, relaxed, space or place. Then during the daytime it shifts again as the sun rises.

Sunsets and sunrises are the clues to the vibrational changes in the atmosphere, which are sleeping and being awake! During these deep REM sleep patterns, you may be carried away by Spirit in order for you to be rejuvenated through its Source of White Light as well as to assist within the Spirit world. This evening time of rest will indeed continue to be a time of rejuvenation but also a time of assisting. However, keep in mind in this original world you will not feel tired or exhausted but will awake refreshed. This is due to the gentle high vibrational quality of energy that is occurring at this time of the planet. Presently you may be assisting in the Spirit world when asleep and perhaps may feel exhausted when you awake. Within the original world, you will not be exhausted due to the higher vibration upon the planet. These are great and spectacular times for all beings of human, nature, Spirit, and energy.

Illusion

Everything is an "illusion" is revealed by this All Truth. You as a human form are an illusion. What this means is that the human form is mainly composed of water and this form is created around the water. The central spiritual core, which is not the illusion, is called *the Essence, the Spirit, the inner self of being or consciousness.* It is within this place where illusion drips away and one is able to see life as it really is – Essence within the form.

The Essence or the stillness is the way in which we perceive everything. This is the way in which all beings *see* life and *feel* life. It is the way in which one lives a life filled with the Spirit or Essence. Life from a perspective of feeling Life! All things derived from the awakened state consist of truly seeing, knowing, and believing all is perfect.

What this really means is, *what is important in life?* You begin to realize that matching pillows or organized silverware in perfect fashion is no longer important. What is important is the way one looks at life and how one sees and feels life. When existing and living from Essence, one then realizes that life is quite simple and everything else doesn't really matter much. This is when you reach a certain point in your life where you begin to feel and believe that life offers so much more, and you believe this to be absolutely right. If you are seeking fulfillment in your life, then you are asking yourself to become engaged in being awakened. This awakened state of being melts away the illusions that have been created by you in life. It removes the illusions or the programmed ideas of life. These programmed ideas of life are those that have been formed by the ego. For example, ego suggests one must possess the most beautiful and expensive car one can buy! Another false belief or illusion is that one must live in the most luxurious, amazingly decorated house. By believing these illusions you fall into the pit of falsehoods. This pit is one of *make-believe,* believing that everything is perfect because you have all the material things you need. You have the big house, expensive car and great job, all of your pillows match, your 100 percent pure silverware is in perfect order and fashion. It needs to be stated that if you do lead an ego-based life of greed, and selfishness, then yes, there is something missing within your way of being. It is the recognition that you are Spirit or Essence. It is the recognition that this is all you are – nothing more – and at this point you realize that with this heightened awareness feeling you will engage in a life filled with meaning. This meaning is the way in which one conducts oneself when living from Essence.

If you are or have been awakened, and life is being revealed to you differently than before, from the Essence or the still perspective, then you will see everything differently. You will no longer use ego to identify you with your objects of beauty. You will see, feel, know, and believe that if you own that large expensive home or drive a very large car then you will be able to see clearly what you need to accomplish through these objects of beauty. It is through your way of seeing and feeling everything that you will be able to use these items of beauty in a most spiritual fashion. It is through this way of being where further ideas of how to serve the planet will surface, perhaps using your spacious, expensive car to drive friends and colleagues to work. It can be as simple as this.

It is not being said that one should not acquire these items of beauty, but when they are acquired they could perhaps be shared and experienced by others as well. It is here in this place one becomes filled with the Essence of being, where all beings are able to complete the fulfillment of their lives in a more comfortable way. What this means is that once one becomes attuned to the way in which life is lead as an awakened being, then one arrives in the knowing of illusion. It is within this illusion when everything is revealed and everything is taken care of. It is here where all falsehoods are then released and a new being is birthed. Arrive here in this place – a place of comfort, peace, joy, serenity, and stillness. Remain here in this place of truth and knowing. It is here within this place whereby all is alive. This place is that which is considered to be One with stillness and nothing more. Material goods will then have different meanings through the eyes and feelings of being awakened. One shall see how this works and how this way of living reveals so much more about life.

Therefore when one steps out of illusion, one then steps into reality, which is Essence. You will never need to look behind you ever again because the only path for you to walk is ahead of you. However, some humans are caught up in illusions. These humans are considered to be filled with illusions and contemplations of ideals that are actually unreal and in fact led by the ego. It is stated that humans are here on this planet to create the breakage of the illusion in order for others to see.

Mother Earth and Father Sky know exactly what the illusion entails and what exactly this means because truth and reality are all it knows – this is it! Mother Earth and Father

Sky have no attachment to anything – nothing! Unlike the human being form. This is fact! Mother Earth and Father Sky live in a different dimension than the human being. They live in complete Essence.

By saying all of this, it is vital that you realize this Crystal Collective message of illusion which states, "this is a time when all beings are exposed to the possibility of being released from the illusions. This will be based upon a feeling level. This feeling is a feeling that is considered to be of greatness in soul and Spirit. It is through this realization that the original world will be created."

Be Set Free

Within the Crystal Collectives of this particular collective is the holding space or place of "greatness of self" as declared by the All Truths. What this means is that the Crystal Collectives are indicating that all human beings have this "self" within them that desires to be set free. This means that all people know exactly what they need to do in life, where to go in life, who they are in life, and more. They already know all of this. Humans already know that life has so much more to offer them and all they need to do is accept and listen to this inner desire or knowing. The desire is actually intertwined in the knowing. It is the core of the knowing.

So for example, an accountant states, "I so desire to become a full-time artist. I so desire to be freer than what I am living in my life right now." It is within this desire that the knowing exists and within the knowing desire exists. This knowing of the desire or the desire of the knowing is always there until you open it up and recognize and realize it for itself and then begin to live it to its absolute fullest potential. If you don't open it up to let it live to its potential, then *desiring* will just become larger, thus forming an emptiness. An empty space of just desiring. When you begin to feel this empty space, you begin to create more desire and more emptiness because desire and emptiness attract more desire and emptiness. This desire creates loneliness, and sadness because one is not listening to one's knowing. More desire is created and is attracted to them.

Move into a life filled with beauty, peace, stillness and passion that you desire—move into this life – your life of knowing! Your life of being that full authentic self. That self you create from who you really, really are. You create that self of love, peace, joy; the authentic you! You create this because you are this – Spirit, authentic you, authentic self. Authentic Oneness with self.

It is time for you to come forward and say, "Here I am. This is who I am!" More beings are coming forward and declaring their truths of who they are, and, as the All Truths indicate, all humans, no matter where they live, have this deep inner knowing of who they are. It is held in a special sacred space within themselves. It is there within themselves. It is where the crystals lie and where they will find all of their answers to their questions, and it is really as simple as this.

"Be you and be only you – nobody else but you. Listen to your knowing because this is where everything lies. This is where all things exist within your knowing."

Oneness of Being

This next Crystal Collective All Truth message deals with the everlasting – "Awakening into the Oneness of *being*." The questions may arise from this question, "How long will I actually be able to maintain this feeling of *being* awakened?" "How long does Spirit last?" If you begin to doubt this feeling, this is when the ego starts to do its nasty business. Ego starts to create as much doubt as possible because it does not like how you become awakened to your Spirit. So to answer the question as posed above – yes! Of course Spirit is unending and never stops. It is unending and is always *is* nothing more and nothing less, *just is*. Spirit is eternal so the feeling of being awakened is just that – eternal. However long you wish it to be, this is your choice and your decision. You decide if you want to believe that the feeling of awareness continues on or does not. If your mind decides, then the ego has a bit of a say on this. However, if your feelings and inner knowing decide, then of course the awareness lasts forever because it is Spirit. Isn't it amazing when you decide what is knowing? Then everything else flows from this.

Spirit is eternal and never ending – always lasting and always here within you – always!

Do not worry or be afraid that Spirit will leave because it won't – ever! Once you begin to feel afraid or worry about this, then this feeling is an *in* for the ego. The ego enjoys suffering! The ego longs and waits for this moment then tries to sneak in. But always remember that you are Spirit – Spirit is you and that is that! As declared by this All Truth.

Akashic Records

I t is stated within the Akashic Records of the universe, for the universe, that everything will shift into the Oneness of self. In other words, everything that is of White Light, beauty, peace-filled, and solid in stillness will understand and in fact know what the depth is for the Akashic Records for the universe.

It is now a time for beings, and this means all beings; (humans, plants, animals, sea creatures, and more) to shift and discover the incredible occurrences taking place on this planet. The energies and Spirits of the prophecies are declaring that the universe now needs to look deeply into its Akashic Records or soul's purpose. This is to discover its next move in this life time in order to complete one of the final phases in its life – thus the shifting is created. It is within this shift that all planets, galaxies, and other worlds that are parallel will exist as One large unit gathered by and through the *arms of love*. It is here in the arms of love that you find the profoundness of all of life. It is here in this point in and of time where the universe's energies or Spirits shift and gently move and allow all that needs to be allowed.

This planet can no longer hold the fear-based feelings that seem to be surrounding the planet and within the planet. What this creates is an energy of tension within the universe and it becomes difficult for the energies to breathe their air of love, life, laughter, and passion. The universe is saying "Enough! Time to shine my light and lights of prophecy." It is now time to arrive in this place. It is now time to fulfill the prophecy of the Akashic Records of the universe.

Time to clear, cleanse, release, *and* allow, believe and know that all is in the perfect tenderness of Spirit. This is now the time from 2012 and post-2012. There are no symbols, secret documents, specific news stories, or books to read. Only just being in the moment – the now of Spirit. This is all – nothing more!

Therefore this particular Crystal Collective All Truth message is from a portion of the crystals that is indicative of the notion or idea of knowing, believing, and allowing! This is the place one needs to enter and remain because it is the place where all things are created. It is within the knowing, believing, and allowing where Spirit works through you. It is here within these pages of knowing, believing, and allowing when one becomes transformed. These pages are those of the Akashic Records – these records are your life so allow these pages to be read, fully explored, and examined. Each being has an individual Akashic Record with Source/God/White Light. This book or record is your entire life from an inner perspective—from a deeper spiritual perspective! This deeper spiritual perspective is one of soul's purpose: who am I, where am I going? These questions and more are answered within the Akashic Record or book of life. The book of life and the book of truths are intricately woven together.

The Akashic Records are the new book of truths or the All Truths of the planet and universe or the original world. This is what the Mayans, Incas, and other wisdom teachers tapped into – the purpose of planet. The universe, all as One. Each Akashic Record of each person coincides with the Akashic Record of the planet. Isn't this amazing, beautiful, and most magnificently planned? You see how this is organized and soulfully and spiritually planned along the line of the crystallized eternity. This means the lines of crystals that create the life line of Spirit within each, thus creating Oneness. This is piecing together slowly, gently, carefully, in perfect order. Each person you see now as you look around you is being slowly, gently, carefully placed within the knowing, believing, and allowing of one's Akashic Record.

Some humans are awakening faster than others and are knowing, and believing that their Akashic Records will unfold in a most perfect fashion. Your records can actually be accessed through your Spirit and some are able to channel their Akashic Records by looking into their sacred space or place of body, mind, soul, heart, and emotion. It is here within these records that all is known and the best part of all of this is you already know who you are, what your purpose is, what you want and dream – you just need to tap into this knowing. Surrounding the knowing is the believing and allowing. Believe in your Spirit – in you. Trusting is the key. Then of course allow your Akashic to come forward in beauty, elegance, and grace.

The All Truths as messaged within the Crystal Collectives are the Akashic Records. More of each person's Akashic Records are being exposed because the veil is thinning and the opening to these records is coordinating with your still point.

To explain this further, when you approach your still point – that point at which you decide to become awakened – you then open up your Akashic Record and these three keys: knowing, believing, and allowing. It is as if a wave of stillness overrides you in a great completeness of movement. This wave of movement is the realization. The realization that there is a grand Source within you that is so beautiful, loving, dearly kind, passionate, and compassionate. Don't you see reader?

This is who you are! Once realized, all doors are opened for you and to you! It is here within the opening where all gifts are gifted to you and you are then ready to allow the acceptance or reception. You see how this works? The veil or your form/body thins as the Spirit becomes larger and, yes, some will say, "But you'll become so ungrounded that you won't be able to function." What this means is that one must still remain intact with what is going on here on Earth – be aware of everything. Do not get carried away too much!

However, when in meditation get carried away and fly with the archangels, angels, and Spirit. Be aware of what is going on always. Be aware of what is happening not only within your own self but exterior of self – your neighborhood, community, town, city, world, planet, and universe. However, if you become too ungrounded you are then too inner to self and can't seem to focus outside self. You may go from one extreme of being in form as an unawakened person to then awakening and being fully inner – in Spirit – very ungrounded. This is natural until a balance occurs because you do need to carry on with relationships, jobs, travel, laundry, cooking, walking, and talking.

Try your best to be in the now and to be balanced. Yes, there may be hours, minutes, seconds, or in some cases days, weeks, or months when being awakened is so overwhelming in beauty that you just want to bask in its flavor of truth. Then you begin to settle into life in order to help out on the planet! You then begin to realize that the impossible is possible and more! This is almost a surreal experience that is quite astounding – when true awakening occurs. This is a most important time in world history, and if you are reading this book then consider yourself extremely lucky! Does luck really exist? It was all planned because no matter how old you are, you have a plan and purpose in the awakening of the planet—of the people!

You are part of the Akashic Record for the planet and are included within these plans and pages of the record. Because all are One – Oneness is the key and the only key as stated within this book of All Truths.

All beings in life coexist together and feel their trueness of self within the energy that shifts and moves itself from one being to the next. It is here where Spirit is found. Each person affects the next person and the next and the next. All are One! If you injure one being, you injure yourself. If you love one being, you love yourself. Therefore if you injure or love yourself first, then you will injure or love others because that is what you believe to be inside of you.

You affect others whether you know this or not. It is happening! We are all One. Be clear and allow no blockages to reign within you. Be aware of everything that you think, feel, and sense. Be aware of the most subtle pieces of yourself. Allow the sun rays to shine through you just like they sparkle through the translucent leaves of the trees. Have you even noticed how the sun shines through leaves as it provides food or chlorophyll in order for the leaf to breathe, eat, live, love, and pray in gratitude to the nurturance of the sun? That is all! How beauty*full* !

If you allow yourself to be separate from others, you are blocked, suffering, doubtful, fear-filled, angry, and/or frustrated. You may be living a life through ego and not of Spirit or Source. This makes you not of Oneness but of *I* – One of self – selfishness or ego. This is not the way to live as One with Spirit. Remember you are One with all people, nature, sea, sky, and earth, and if you so decide to live from suffering then you are living in separation because this is what you have been told by the ego – the ego so loves it when you believe that you are separate from others and it places you in an illusion that perhaps you are not worthy. This is when loneliness and feeling you don't belong begins to grow. People then become detached physically, energetically, and spiritually from all beings. They may develop greed, deceit, self-absorption, dysfunctional relationships, and broken job opportunities. Little do they know they are all One and they will affect all beings around them, energetically and physically because we are all One. Therefore, be caring, be loving, be joyful within and to yourself – watch the ego and live life to its fullest of Divine peace and the solidity of stillness.

In order for the Akashic Records of the planet to be read and opened completely at a high vibrational frequency, human beings are required to awaken. All is in perfect plan and order as the Akashic Records or the All Truths from the Crystal Collectives are being exposed and realized.

These Akashic Records can also be considered as maps that are of life and the original world. Maps that are spiritually bound or contained therefore create beauty. These maps are spiritual maps, which are the words, tones, phrases, feelings, energies, and spiritual existences placed carefully upon the pages of the Akashic Records or the Crystal Collectives. Same thing. Crystal Collectives = Akashic Records. All messages are connected via the maps of the words, tones, phrases, feelings, energies, and spiritual existences as gently placed within the universe. The crystals from the Crystal Collectives are throughout you, the earth, the atmosphere, Spirit, energy(ies), nature – everywhere – and they are intensifying their energy. The Spirit is intensifying itself as well. Which is why *more* people are awakening, the veil is thinning, there is more discussion about ego and purpose.

This *more* is the meaning of what is really going on, which is the following: all beings are slowly emerging into the Spirit/Source of White Light. Source is calling all beings back to the original world. This transition is coming closer and in a most slow and beautiful way. This is what is happening!

This is what is occurring today and has been since the beginning of the transitioning into the Oneness – the unmanifested – the stillness. All beings are moving and shifting back to the original. You need to realize that the ego does not wish for you to awaken to your Spirit. It will try hard to contain you in fear, darkness, self-doubts, and worthlessness. The ego is the darkness. It seeks the flesh – the form – the material. It has served its purpose and now is the time to no longer listen to its chatter, its fear, its depression, or anxiety because it is desperately attempting to separate you from your spiritual existence.

Some decide to listen and even worship the ego to the extent where ceremonies are prepared in the worship of the dark as an extreme case, or you may just simply be addicted to fear, anger, low self-worth, etc. This is still the darkness – the ego – whatever name you call it. Pay attention! Do not believe its lies, untruths, and seductions. It is trying to hold you captive. Remember this is impossible when you realize that you are Spirit and are Oneness and all you need to do is know, allow, and believe this to be so.

Will Power

The Crystal Palace, which is filled with the Crystal Collectives, is an energy place of deep serenity and contemplation. It is a place of will and the freedom to choose this *will*, being of course *will power*. This means that all humans have the power to choose anything in life – that anything may be the choice to live that is defined through the central core of self named Spirit or that which is defined through separateness or movement away from the White Light Spirit, which is named ego.

Some people are simply choosing to not live from this White Light place – love is always available to everybody who chooses love. Love and the purity of love is always, and in *all ways*, available to all. If you don't choose love, then you don't choose love. But pay close attention to what happens within your life when you do choose to live from love. The purity of love will gather around because you have chosen this and you have decided this is your way of being. Relax into this way of being, and when you do contain and maintain this lifestyle then everything will flow from this so much so that the universe or the spiritual law of attraction will say, "Here is more for you." Because you will be attracting more of the same. It is as simple as this!

Redemption of Self

This next Crystal Collective is one of the All Truths that will connect each person to his or her "redemption of self." What this means is his/her connection to the greatness of whom he/she is already. In realizing that as one shifts into the awakened realized self, one shifts into who they already are. By redeeming or surrendering oneself, you then become empty of all that is of pain and suffering because you redeem this negativity and lower vibrational energy. You shift and move these parts out of your body and become emptied of these lower vibrations and filled with that of higher vibrations. In other words, you become filled with that of who you already are. This is the best part and you see when you release these lower vibrational pieces of self you then create the space or the emptiness for the true self to shine forth or forward. You allow that which is you – your Spirit – to move forward and for you to freely live within this space or place in time. When you have released your pain and suffering, you are redeeming yourself and you are saying to the Spirit, "I am now ready to move forward in my life and to be that shining bright light for all to see. This is who I already am." The releasing of the need for pain and suffering then causes the real easing that allows you to maintain yourself in the flow of all that is of love, joy, peace, bliss, and more.

The redemption of self is the moment or the still point by which you say, "I am redeemed" or "I surrender into that place of peacefullness." Within this place of emptiness, assuredness or this place of completeness of self you may ask, "Is it here where I find my authentic self? It is here I find who I am and what life means for me?" The redemption of self is entering that part of you that is maintained by your Spirit – that which is the Spirit. Arise to greet your Spirit with joy, laughter, bliss, excitement, and more because within the redemption is the real-*easing*. It is the self that is Spirit – nothing more.

Surrender and redeem self into that place of who you really are. Nothing more than this! Therefore the redemption of self is the returning to the original self and acquiring all that is filled with love. Redemption is just releasing, letting go, surrendering of what you do not wish to maintain or contain within you anymore.

Redemption therefore is that still point. That in-between space of creation and stillness. It is that place where you create your stillness and where you create a still point of releasing. You then create that which needs to be acquired, which is the act of realizing you are already enlightened. Therefore realizing you are already there and ready to shift or transition your life. It is now time for you to become who you really are—redeem yourself into that being of who you are already. One of great stillness and tranquility, gently transitioning into that place.

Health

This Crystal Collective is indicating that 2012 and onward, you will begin to experience fewer illnesses or diseases, such as cancer, multiple sclerosis, colds, flu, and others, due to the higher vibrational frequency of the planet. What this means is that as more people come to be awakened and raise their energetic vibrational frequency, this then also increases the planet's vibrational frequency. With this raising of the frequency, the human forms take on a healthy, clearer, and cleaner energetic connection to Spirit. The human then needs to believe itself as being whole, loving, bliss-filled, and healthy. Take hold of the White Light of Source and say, "This is who I am! Healthy, well, fit, and engaged in Spirit."

When this connection or awakening is made with many people, you will see cancer decreasing as well as other illnesses and even just colds, flu, rashes, and so much more because dis-ease cannot and will not live within a form resonating at a higher energetic frequency. This is indeed a mystic law or All Truth.

If, however, you do become touched with a dis-ease or illness while within your living of being awakened, pay attention to its message, because it has a message for you. Listen to its message and let it go of dis-ease completely. It is within your spiritual connection where the cleansing, clearing, and rejuvenating will occur. And it really is as simple as this! One just needs to believe, allow, and know this to be true. This is the way to freedom! This is the way to dissolve within yourself any form of dis-ease and to create only ease – an easing of life. A careful way of being! This word *careful* just means *gentle* – *a gentle way of being* – nothing more than this! It becomes very clear and evident that when you begin to explore the emotional/ spiritual disconnect and the reasons behind dis-ease you then have further awakenings of being a being of Spirit.

Re-storing and Re-shuffling

The Crystal Collectives within the All Truths are spoken from within their forms of crystallized scrolled messages in such a way that when the messages are released a grand energetic affair occurs. This means you already have an innate ability to restore all that needs to be restored. It is from this place in your heart, where this treasure to create more space to restore is of the utmost importance for your life.

What needs to be reshuffled and restored in order for you to move onward and forward in life? Is it something that needs to be transformed or transitioned into something new? Does it need to be restored from a heart perspective?

There comes a certain point in some people's lives when a shuffle, recleansing, or restocking is in order. This is required in order for you to shift your vibration to a higher level and to move onward and forward. It is here within this reshifting and reshuffling where you discover *your truth*. You discover your way of being and who you are. Begin to reshuffle and restore your life and bring forward those pieces of yourself and then see what happens. There is power and empowerment within reshuffling, restoring, or restocking of self. You shall see!

This is an extremely important All Truth message because it is showing you the absolute vital inner core message that needs to shine through you, which is "reshuffle, restock, and then restore that which is of a high vibrational way of being."

Feel Love at Its Fullest

This next Crystal Collective has the message of love and beauty. *Love and beauty* means that you begin to choose carefully what you allow into your life. The crystals energetically state that you may love someone but this love may be a love of material world and form. It is a love that may be numb of true beauty within this feeling called love, which means you may love someone according to your agenda or an ego love, an intellectual love not one of beauty, passion, and compassion.

The Crystal Collectives are messaging love to you and what this feels like at a very deep level of self when awakened. You will feel, taste, smell, touch, and hear the beauty within love. It is a feeling that cannot be described in any language or words of any form.

When awakened, the feeling or energy of love blossoms forth and you can become so open to love of and for yourself that others will want what you have, which in fact is in all people. Don't be afraid of love – you see where there is fear there is no love, and where there is love there is no fear – simple!

You decide – you make a choice to live from love and so be it! This means that life is filled with beauty everywhere. Even in the following example there is beauty; when two parents lose a child at birth to its next life as Spirit. As one awakens to love, you know that this needed to occur for some reason. This reason may never be known or it may be known. No matter, when awakened in the purity of love you see, feel, taste, touch, and smell all of the beauty within everything. As stated in previous sections, this doesn't mean you don't feel hurt, pain, or sorrow – you do feel these feelings, but you feel them intertwined in a feeling of the beauty of knowing and acceptance. You see how this works? The Crystal Collectives All Truths message in energetic/spiritual form is indicating to you that being the reflection of love, allows you to see beauty in everything. To maintain this feeling of love is simple.

Just accept it as a way of life.
Just allow it to move through you.
Just believe you are love – how could you not
be because you are created from love.
Just know that when in love, more beauty will be
shown to you – more will arrive into your life.

People, please listen and feel this message of Divine truths or the All Truths because you see all you need to do is allow, believe, and know that you are love – you are God! That's it – that's all!

Therefore when you ask the question, "Well, okay how can I maintain this feeling?" You just know, believe, and allow. What you are sending out to the universe is what will come back to you – always!

When in love, it will come back to you completely!

Read and reread this discussion over and over again until it resonates deeply within you. When you enter into a life of love and experience the stillness within this love, you will never turn back. You will never return to the place you were before. Ever! The inner stillness of love is comprised of beauty and peace, which resonates through your entire life and self. You then know, feel, believe, allow, and experience peace. When you choose peace, you also then are choosing love. Love and peace are inseparable feeling energies – they wrap around each other with a bow of beauty!

Don't look back!

Take Deep Care of Yourself

This next Crystal Collective scribed All Truth is of greatness in the deep care of self. "Taking care of oneself is of utmost importance and requires that you remain steadfast within who you are." Let go of everything that you have attached yourself to. This could be a dysfunctional relationship or perhaps the attachment has caused the dysfunction. Also let go of attachments to material wealth or status symbols. Some people may even be attached to negative emotions, such as fear, anger and frustration.

Realize also when the Crystal Collectives are saying, "Care deeply within yourself and be free and easy of who you are. Be tender with yourself and indulge in silence and stillness. Indulge in who you really are and focus on what you will bring to this planet. Indulge in your Spirit." Allow your Spirit to shine forth and upon our planet, especially now in these times of great change. In these times of great shifting and transitioning, be glad in all that is occurring within Spirit. Be glad that as you indulge within yourself you are letting go of everything and reconnecting to Spirit – that is all.

The All Truths indicate that now is the time to indulge within your Spirit. Now is the time to create that life which needs to be created in order for Spirit to move through you. Within the spiritual form of existing, it is a time for healing, shifting, or letting go of everything you have put in your way – letting go of all that is of unrest and of unrealities. Allow yourself to acquire the Essence of who you are and where you are coming from and where you are going. You are in fact already where you need to be and you are already in a most beautiful place in time. Indulge yourself in Spirit as all comes from this place of spiritual indulgence. This is not gluttony or greed but a tender, easy indulgence. A form of loving easily and gently. A form of peacefulness that is contemplative and a resilience to stay within that feeling. A gentle, easy way or form of existing – indulging in Spirit – that's all!

Divine Intervention

This next Crystal Collective represents the scribed message from the All Truths that is of Divine "intervention." What you will see and experience are incidents of Divine interventions. These will be noticed by you immediately when you have been awakened and, in fact, these Divine interventions or synchronicities are occurring moment by moment. When you awakened you will notice, feel, see, and create all Divine interventions or Divine synchronicities every millisecond of the day.

When awakened you realize:

You are a Divine intervention

You are Spirit

You are Source/God

You are love

You are peace

You are bliss

You are grace

You are stillness

This is you!

You have just been programmed and conditioned to believe otherwise – that's all. You have been told what and who you are by many people, including yourself, and you have believed all of it, and we are talking about programmed illusions such as the following:

- Not enough
- Not worthy
- Not healthy
- Not good
- Nobody will love me
- And so on

Why do you still believe these programmed illusions? They are saying that you do not respect nor do you believe, know, and allow the Spirit to work through you? Remember that you are Source/Spirit/God – you are this! When you allow the Light to shine through you, this Divine Light of intervention will move and slide through your entire self to all people.

This intervention of the Divine occurs millisecond by millisecond every day – every single day, never ending unless *you* stop this from occurring. Be aware that, when awakened, it is vital for you to give thanks, praise, and gratitude to all interventions whenever you notice them. Or at the glorious and sweet end of the day, simply say, "Thank you God/Source/ Spirit for this miraculous day." Divine intervention is available continuously as stated earlier, to all people – those awakened and those not awakened.

To those not awakened, these interventions will become louder, stronger, more powerful in tone because Spirit/Divine Source is trying to relay a message to you, and if you can't sense the message then it becomes louder and louder until you hear, feel, taste, touch, or even smell the message. For example, if you experience slight abdominal pain but refuse to listen to its message, then, as the Divine works, the message will become stronger and louder until you have no choice but to listen to or feel the message. When you have Divine interventions, pay attention to the message. This pain is trying to convey its message.

Listen, feel, touch, and be aware of everything that is going on around you – all the time. Be in the now. Be present! Be here! When awakened, you are continually aware of everything all the time – never do you stop being aware. As a result you see, feel, hear, taste, touch, and smell these interventions in their fullness of strength.

> *Know* that Divine interventions are
> occurring every single millisecond.
> *Believe* that Divine interventions are
> occurring every single millisecond.
> *Allow* these Divine interventions to
> occur every single millisecond.

When you create the awareness of these Divine interventions and say thank-you and live in bliss, harmony with Spirit, the grace and the law of attraction will work its magic because you will attract more of the same because what you are saying to the universe is what you want – and the universe will give more of what you are asking for – this is truth!

When unawakened and walking through life on automatic pilot or thinking in future terms, then the universe will give you more and more of this awakened state. But do remember that the Divine interventions will occur for you. They are messaging to you. If awakened, you hear, see, feel, taste, smell, and/or touch the message. Learn from the message and move deeper into oneself. Then more will come your way. If unawakened, then you may have a message or Divine intervention that simply needs to become louder and louder until you hear the message.

Divine is what and who you are and your purpose or soul's purpose is to intervene on this planet with your message of love to all people. This message of love is the Divine clearly working through you and for you. Allow the Divine to work through you to intervene and be that open instrument or vessel of love, peace, stillness, bliss, passion, grace, and compassion. You, the Divine, created by the Divine or Source must then speak, touch, and create love everywhere. Spreading love throughout the planet is your purpose.

Be your Divine intervention! Be who you are! Nothing other than you! Nothing untrue, nothing false, nothing illusory, nothing other than love, peace, bliss, joy, compassion, passion, and grace.

Electrical Patterns

The energy patterns will also be changing dramatically in the next number of years. The energy's electrical patterns will be shifting and performing differently when producing electricity. The original world is going to utilize electricity via the energetic patterns of energy. Since the thinning of the veil is occurring over the next number of years, it will become apparent that there is a different form of electricity, being produced through this Spirit connection and is unseen but will be available.

As the environment cleanses itself and rejuvenates itself, electricity will be brought forward as a topic of concern. Currently the concern is that we are running low on electricity and this affects its applications and implementation. Therefore different designs have been developed. We have solar, wind, and other forms of power. What will occur according to the Crystal Collectives All Truth is the fact that a new discovery will be made allowing us to tap into the energy electrical force or Source automatically. All it will take is a special type of tool or metal instrument that is able to plug into a vortex, and there will be several available.

A vortex is a power force or source of energy. There are several around the planet but nobody has figured out how to tap into its energy to create the electrical power. There are, however, many more White Light vortexes being created throughout the entire planet that will be available for electricity usage. These vortexes are available because of the thinning of the veil as well as the vibrational increases, which as stated several times, stems from you as the human being.

Electrical power through the energy vortexes or through other sources of nature, such as sun, and wind, and even the rain, will be continued to be explored and utilized as forms of energy for all to use.

The Children of Those Awakened

This next Crystal Collective All Truth deals with the fact that "when one is living in the realms of being awakened, then his/her children will also become fully awakened." The children who descend from the awakened parents will already be engaged within the state of being awakened – or transformed. When you awaken in this life time, you then have an influence upon others and some of these *others* may be those who are bearing children. When these children are born, they are completely living within the stance of being awakened due to the fact that their parents are also awakened. When awakened to the realization that you are already enlightened, just imagine the impact this has upon the children – perhaps your children.

Even if you do not have children, but are awakened, you still psychically influence the energy of the planet because of your vibrational increase. As you increase your vibration and travel more deeply into the awakened state, you are still influencing all beings whether you birth children or not. Many children are being born who are considered to be the helpers, healers, assistors, and assistants in shifting the planet back to its original state of being – the original world.

This All Truth is also stating, "Children are being prepared to be born in order to assist in the transition to the full metamorphosis stage of 3012." The beginning of all of this is occurring now until 2014 – this is the shift of preparing, the stage one of changes along the spiritual evolutionary line of now's. It is then followed by 2014 until the end of 2018, where the transition stage changes begin slowly to occur, and then 2019 and years after the metamorphosis begins.

Children will be born to assist in the careful transition of the movement toward the completed metamorphosis of 3012, which means within these hundreds of years many Homo-Luminous beings will be born. They will be arriving and their soul purpose is to assist within this the transitioning into the full metamorphosis stage.

These next hundreds of years will be most fascinating and exciting. It is the returning to the original state of being and now is the time to start to prepare and transition.

What else will begin to occur and needs to occur soon, is the shift in schooling. Educational styles, theories, philosophies, and teaching strategies for children about emotions, kindness to others, and no bullying will shift. Each person is different, and how each person is Spirit is just starting to be taught in some small private schools with a spiritual focus while other schools are just beginning to speak about character and feelings. As 2012 approaches, you will see more of these teachings and hear more about the language of Spirit being used.

These times are tremendously exciting. If a leader or principal of a school or head of many schools is awakened, then this person will be able to influence the entire school and staff of teachers, including a new curriculum of philosophies, and strategies. This will occur over time as more people within the school systems become aware of the true feeling and meaning of life. It is and can be as simple as this. As more parents become awakened and live within the now moment, they too will be influencing the school and the boards of education.

Become enwrapped in the awakened state in order to help the children – the future of the planet. They too need to be awakened and engaged within the promises of the transition and metamorphosis through the evolutionary stages of Spirit.

Just reading this book will assist you in raising your awareness. In fact, you don't even need to read this book, just have it lying around and its energetic vibration will influence your energetic vibration.

Unknown Is the Known

This Crystal Collective is the Crystal Collective whose All Truth message simply engages the *unknown*, which is really the *known*. When explained, this means as the planet moves through space spiritually, energetically, soulfully, and physically, it is shifting and evolving in such a way that it is in perfect harmony and unison with its way of being. Anything arising or changing or evolving from one millisecond to the next millisecond is of grand goodness.

You see, the planet knows the unknown – the Spirit knows the unknown – all beings know the unknown. So when the question arises; where are we going in this new original world? Know that it comes from the mind/the ego/the suffering instead of *I know that everything will be okay and fine and in complete harmony and love with Spirit/Source/God.* As all beings evolve into that Homo-Luminous form, we then begin to arrive where we were originally: the original world, Spirit.

As all shift and evolve spiritually into a form of formlessness, we arrive then into a state of complete awareness of self. It is within this knowing that everything is perfect and okay. Discover trust and faith. Note that as you travel along your own path or journey into your Homo-Luminous form, everything will become clearer. You will begin to see things differently and in a very different order of being or living. Arrive then into this state of just being in faith, in trust, and you shall see, feel, hear, taste, touch, and smell how everything is falling into place.

Open your eye chakra, ear chakra, heart, solar plexus, and all chakras, and begin to feel the intensity of reasons – reasons of Spirit. Meaning, what is *is!* The unknowns of this spiritual shifting have been known by Spirit since the beginning of time or since the original world, which is where all beings are slowly and beautifully shifting back to. It is within the beauty where the unknown resonates and rests in the palm of the hands of Source. The All Truths say, "Do not worry. Do not fret. Do not create something that is not needed. Continue to live a life of simplicities and ease. Become all you can become in this lifetime. Arise to the occasion of being in touch with all of your selves fully, and engage in all that matters spiritually."

Feel Nature

This next Crystal Collective is one that will message to you through the All Truth about how to live with a passion and compassion for life. What this means is that when aware and living an awakened state, you immediately become filled with passion and compassion for life and all living things. From a tiny speck of sand to a grand mountain standing at 20,000 feet, you develop compassion and passion for all of nature – including those plants called weeds. You see, one can become deeply close to nature when one lives from passion and compassion. You actually will be able to feel and hear all of what nature speaks or messages to you easily.

When you live from compassion and passion, you open up your heart chakra and nature knows this immediately and will gift you beautiful, meaningful messages. Even the songs of birds will resonate within oneself. The songs of the birds, when felt and listened to, resonate and speak with your Spirit. In fact, this is what Spirit sounds and feels like – that beautiful feeling when you are listening to a song bird. Therefore when living your passion and compassion for life, you will truly hear and feel the message. The song bird's music will not just be a song but a message either for you personally or for you to share. It may be a feeling that you need to share or perhaps words or one word. When living intertwined in passion and compassion, life and nature open up wide for you. How wonderful for you! As the veil thins between the material solid form and Spirit, all beings begin to intertwine in purpose through passion and compassion. When you display compassion and passion, then all of nature will naturally mirror this back to you!

And then messages will flood into your life. You need to feel passion and compassion for yourself first and foremost, and all else resonates from here. What you do is open up the channels to all possibilities to occur for you in all ways possible through nature! Nature speaks.

What is also occurring today and forward into the future is that nature will shift and move. This phenomena has been stated several times within the context of the book, concerning the movement within nature. This means the tectonic plates will be slowly shifting, causing landscape changes, rotations of earth as well as the sun, stars, and the moon. The four directions (north, south, east, and west) will slide into different directions. Rain and snow (all precipitation) will also shift their mineral composition. The colors of nature will also shift dramatically into different hues and, more importantly, the Homo-Luminous body of all of nature is slowly evolving. A rainbow in the sky, as you recognize it will no longer appear like a rainbow due to the shift in the Earth's axis and the shifting of the moons and their atmosphere. The rainbow will shift its shape to horizontal rather than curved. This sounds extremely strange, but it is true. This shifting of shape and direction of the rainbow will create some interesting stirs within people because it will confirm and it will be a sign that the earth's rotation, atmosphere, and its axis are shifting and changing. The Spirit of Source is beginning to move through nature. As we shift through 2012 and beyond, all begin to see and feel differently.

Move into your compassion and passion of all of nature and feel what happens. When in this state, you tap into your *isness* and the *isness* of all of nature. You begin to realize that your *isness* is the same *isness* as a tree, flower, rock, friend, and person beside you on the subway. This isness is the Source attached to your authentic self. All beings have the same isness that is Source, but each person expresses it differently because each person has an authentic self expression. Source moves through you in a most Divine way, thus creating passion and compassion.

Waves of Beingness

Among all of these Crystal Collective All Truths are the *waves of beingness*. When one shifts into the awakened state, one then becomes part of the wave. This wave is the wave of energy or Spirit changing, shifting, flowing, and moving into a new dimension. You will sense this shifting occurring because you will become more aware of each piece of life as each piece of life reveals itself slowly to you. These revelations are those that become filled with Divine interventions. Okay, what does this all mean?

It means this: when one becomes awakened to the stillness and the peacefulness that one already is, then one arrives upon the waves of energies that shift, move, and flow throughout the universal container of Spirit. This container of Spirit slowly waves back and forth. As the vibration changes, more waves are created and the stronger they become. In other words, these waves will then slowly yet swiftly roll the energy(ies) or wave the vibration in order to increase the energetic vibration, therefore influencing the planet. When one person realizes something about a realized message, that person is then considered to be riding the wave of the higher vibration. As these waves continue and are created by the rising vibration of each being, then the more realizations will exist and develop further.

When riding the waves of energy, you will slowly or quickly develop more and more realizations. For example, when flowing or gently rolling in a wave, you will begin to live more in a present *now* state and notice that synchronicities occur all of the time and the Divine intervention is just another name for synchronicities. Divine interventions or synchronicities actually occur one millisecond after another millisecond. These interventions or synchronicities are not only a way of thinking or your thought patterns but are also comprised of your feelings and emotions.

As you move into your wave of energy, you shift or drift into a wave of being present now and you begin to realize that life is just simply flowing with your waves of energy. How you proceed through your day then is to flow with your intuition or Spirit, and when here, you will be within the wave of energy. When you are within the wave of energy you are then flowing from your heart, which then is followed by the mind, thought, the thinking in order to fulfill the flow. Thus you are flowing and drifting within the waves of life. It really is that simple. You will discover this as you become more attuned to the *now!* To the realization of the present moment.

Flow!
Drift!
Shift!
Attune!

Other Dimensions

Become fully and magnificently aware of what is happening within the world and the world of other dimensions. This Crystal Collective's message from this All Truth states, "As the vibration of the planet increases, this leads to an energetic vibrational increase within other dimensions as well." These other spiritual dimensions include those which are connected to Source but within different dimensions, those which are within the lives of all beings. There are different levels and dimensions within the Spirit world as well, just like there are different dimensions within the human being. You have the human form, Spirit, esoteric field, energy vibrations, and more all streaming from the human being.

As the energetic vibration increases, these dimensions will increase their influence of vibration and in fact their differences in layers will as well. In other words, these several dimensions will begin to become *one dimension* with Spirit instead of several separate dimensions. This is a pattern that is holding true for humans too. When in an awakened state, one then shifts his/her awareness to Spirit – that which they are – and when the awakening occurs all that is Spirit will evolve into a completeness of self. This is called the Homo-Luminous body which is a form of Spirit and exudes this energy that is powered by tremendous and wondrous love.

The human just needs to allow this awakening to occur and then everything stems from this point. The spiritual dimensions shift and become One. Then the Homo-Luminous body begins to emerge and immerse itself into the realities of your life. This may sound confusing to you at first, if you need an illustration to see what one dimension looks like or the Homo-Luminous body refer to Alex Grey's illustrations in his book entitled *Sacred Mirrors: The Visionary Art of Alexander Grey*. His illustrations clearly reveal the magnificence of the Homo-Luminous Spirit form.

What is occurring is that all of life is shifting and reshifting in order for all people to become aware of what is really going on here! Spirit is emerging and all people are being prepared for this awakening. Now is the time to recognize that you are the shift into the newness of now. You are it! This is one of the most important All Truths.

Women and Men

As more humans become awakened, many realizations will occur and one of them is that more females are sensitive to the awakening than males. Have you noticed that perhaps you as a female reading this book are the one telling your partner/husband/male family member or friend about its spiritual message? Have you ever attended a conference/workshop/lecture on Spirit and most of the participants are females? Why are more females becoming awakened than males? What is happening? For centuries females have been emotionally and spiritually more connected and aware. In fact, if you were to speak with many therapists, counselors, psychiatrists, and psychologists, most of their clients are females sorting through their issues they believe they are carrying.

How many times has a female stated, "I am growing beyond my husband/partner and leaving him behind; what shall I do?" The female inevitably will leave spiritual books lying around the house concerning authentic self, purposes in life, Spirit, and relationships. Sometimes the male will listen and accept, sometimes not. Females seem to be the spiritual leaders on this planet due to their *Crystal Collective cellular make-up*. Many males are as well, and in fact some of the most influential spiritual leaders presently in this field or time of awakening are men. However the majority of the awakened people on the planet are female. They are also joining together as groups or gatherings to discuss and connect at deep spiritual levels. Women are telling other female friends and family so more females are *unfolding*. For some reason, the male is having a harder time letting go of the ego, laws, rules, and regulations. It seems to be a harder concept for men to feel, believe, know, and allow themselves to live a life of being awakened. However, once they are, they do not waiver or question and in fact will change their lives completely. Whereas the female may sometimes question a bit, need to discuss further with female friends, collect further guidance from others, yet the male will not do this when awakened! He will move forward quite quickly.

Females are more connected to the belly of Mother Earth through nurturance. This means being more emotionally connected, which is a stronger and clearer connection to Spirit – to flowing with life – to the Oneness in life. It is here the female awakening occurs. The male being is more strongly connected to Father Sky because the Father holds everything in place – he is the strength of the stars, as the male being has been led to believe for centuries that he is the strength of the family. He has to hold everything together. However, pay attention to the following: without Mother Earth, there would be no plants, animals, earth, or food. Without Father Sky there would be no sun, sky, stars, or galaxies, which are all needed to help grow vegetation which serves as food for the animals. In other words, sure the male and the female humans may have some similar qualities of the Mother and the Father, but both are equal. One is not stronger or better than the other – both are the same.

The illusion that the male needs to be stronger, more forceful, more confident in ego and maintaining the identity of who he is, and soon to consider himself in control of his life and family is a falsehood. This is just another one of those programmed ideas, opinions, and thoughts from centuries ago. And it still is alive today.

Since more females than males are awakening, as already stated, the vibration of the planet will increase, thus causing a softness upon the planet as the feminine energy of nurturance is revealed. What this means then is that, as the vibration increases, then males will feel this energetically and slowly awaken themselves. Because of how they have been programmed not only genetically but through thoughts, ideas, and opinions, they still believe that "control and ego" are important. However, as you can see this is slowly changing or evolving for the male and more men are now attending conferences, workshops, and lectures. Yes, perhaps it is because the female has pushed them to attend – yet some do go on their own accord. Slowly this is occurring as men just begin to see and feel the impact that awakening is having upon their partners, wives, friends, and female family members. Men are being required to hear and feel these women differently and know that, as the shift continues to evolve and approach, more women will be transitioning. They are beginning to see and feel something differently. This is all in perfect plan and order. There are no mistakes within this spiritual world evolution.

There are females and males being born today already awakened and are gathering together. The children who are being born during these times and in the past few years are Indigo, Crystal, Atlantis, Star children, Rainbow children, and others. They are being born and recognized as different from other children because of what they know and their obvious psychic abilities. They are here and ready to assist within this evolutionary spiritual transition. They are able to understand

and feel at a very deep crystal way of being. These children are born with their crystal cells already awakened and activated.

Keep in mind and heart that women must realize that they need to keep going – don't stop moving more deeply into their awakened state just because their partner (either male or female) is not awakened. Women will just keep going, knowing that all is in perfect alignment and in perfect order. Sure more females are awakened than males, but this is beginning to shift in these next few years – in fact a dramatic shift will occur.

When people have awakened they have sparkling eyes and a twinkle, you know who they are. They are extremely still and *move in their stillness.* They connect to nature at a very deep way or level. They flow and shift in life. They are able to move through anything in life in grace and ego free. They are awakened and their energy is greatly influencing the planet. As more and more people – both male and female – become attuned to being awakened, then and only then can the planet become rejuvenated and cleared. It is here within the cleansing and rejuvenating where others will feel the difference and then possibly decide that awakening is the way to live or move. It is within the role modeling of others that others will shift into their awakened state!

So just believe, know, and allow yourself to move in the stillness and keep moving because your role modeling is speaking volumes to all people whom you encounter.

Death and the Thinning of the Veil

The Crystal Collective of this All Truth is indicating in a strong message that "as the veil thins, death will look and feel differently." It will be a feeling of engaging with the *fullest* of the White Light Source. It will be the most amazing experience you have ever encountered in any form.

Death as you hear or read about or perhaps, you have experienced as a near death incident yourself, will appear much different than ever before. As the veil thins in 2012 and onward, it allows the human form availability to step into the Spirit world. It allows you to communicate with the Spirit world fluidly and easily. Allowing you to communicate with those family members or friends who have crossed over. Other human beings who have also crossed over may also be available to you as well, such as Abraham Maslow, Da Vinci, and Michelangelo.

When your body ceases to exist in this form and your Spirit or your Essence leaves or returns to its Creator, then you are able to define how you, as Spirit, would like to be recreated or created once again. Within this energy or Spirit form you know or understand what you need to do, will it be a reincarnation back into a human form or a different style of form, perhaps you will remain within the Spirit realm.

You will be so familiar with the feeling of Spirit that, when crossing into this form of intense existence, you may wish to remain within this Spirit form rather than be reincarnated.

However, remember also those who are choosing to be reincarnated during these next few years are coming back to help – they are coming back to assist in creating and recreating the planet back to its original world.

Another most amazing point for you to feel and read about is that, as the veil thins, then all people actually have more access to all Spirits, archangels, angels, Spirit guides, and friends/family members who have crossed over. The telepathic communication, channeling, or transition of messages will be high and strongly available to all people. So much so that you will see in the next number of years more people coming forward with business or consultations with Spirit because they are channeling or receiving messages for people. This will become very common. But remember that when you are living within your now human form, you can even receive messages from any human being who has passed to the spiritual world of existing, which really is a parallel source or energy force field – there is nothing surreal or fantastical about this at all. If, for example, you are an artist and wish to tap into Leonard Da Vinci to channel some creative visuals, ideas, or inventions, then do so and see if his Spirit is available to you. What this may mean is that all beings who have crossed over may be available according to what they need to accomplish in Spirit form. Some beings may not be available to message you as yet, but continue to try.

As the veil thins, more people will be having conversations about these Spirit-filled messages from the White Light Source of love. These times will be intriguing. However, maintain yourself in a grounded way of existing always because, as the veil thins, it will become easy to be ungrounded due to all of the spiritual connections occurring. Remain grounded, steadfast, and sure within yourself.

The place or this space where all beings return to or shift after the form has expired is a parallel Spirit world of where you exist now. As you read these words, you are in a human form, but when out of human form and existing in the pure spiritual form or non-form you are living as a Spirit within a parallel White Light existence. This parallel existence is parallel to the human form or any solid form. This non-form is resonating at such a high frequency that the feeling is one of peace, love, bliss, and a grand solidity of stillness. This existence is one of greatness and the purest of Spirit. One cannot achieve this feeling within one's present form because of the lower vibration of the human form. However when the human form is deceased then this most amazing Spirit body reveals itself. It is where everything becomes clear.

Do not worry or fret or become anxious over the issue of crossing over because this existence in the Spirit body is most incredible.

Each human life has a Spirit within it, which decides, as written within the soul's contract, when one's physical human form will expire – perhaps at the age of two, fourteen, fifty, sixty, seventy or even one hundred. Each being is here to serve to the best of his or her ability.

This is truly one of the most exciting, emotional, bliss-filled, loving times in history. Live this life as a Spirit in human form in a most beautiful way!

New White Light Workers

Jesus, Buddha, Lao Tzu, and other ascended masters are making themselves known as the veil thins between the Spirit world and form. As well as the archangels, angels, and others are making themselves available more readily and clearly. *More readily* means more accessible for all people in a very clear way. This means or implies that their energy, Spirit, and messages are able to be channeled or transmitted through humans in a clear and concise manner. This is most exciting as the ascended masters are coming forward to assist in the creation of this new way of being. What their message conveyed to all means is to: "Become who you already are, come into the realization that you have arrived, and live from this arrival."

The ascended masters are etched within the crystal catacombs of life for all beings as evidenced through the All Truths. Within these catacombs of ascended masters are more masters coming forward. These masters are exposing or are being reincarnated into human form. They are coming forward in order to assist with the transition and the metamorphosis phase and beyond. It is time! This arrival will become evident when people begin to talk in groups, heal, and just engage in a life filled with bliss and love. You will recognize them and know them right away. Some of them will remain in Spirit energy form and some will be reincarnated as humans (some are here now). As the vibration of the planet's energy increases this allows for further possibilities of the shifting of the original world – Earth of Origin.

Also, become aware that *new* archangels are being created and recreated in order to assist with this transitional and the metamorphosis phase. Presently during this preparation phase, from now until 2014, they are being created. New angels and other White Light Spirit guides are also being created. The White Light of Source is creating and recreating all that is resonating White Light of Love.

These new archangels are presently making themselves known as archangels strong in both male and female energies. They are protectors and healers encompassing all that is of a quiet, serene, and gentle love. Other archangels are those who are here to maintain and contain the stillness of the energies as the *preparation* continues for the readiness of the *transition* and finally the *metamorphosis.*

More angels are being created and recreated in order to assist with the *three phases* as well. White Light of Love has been and continues to be engaged in creating an angelic/spiritual support system for all to tap into. These truly are exciting times for all!

Deliverance of Deserving

This Crystal Collective's All Truth is indicating the following: "when one reaches the awakened state of being, then one truly begins to actualize realizations of love and peace into place." The realization that when you as the *realized* one of love and peace recognizes the *isness* of self you then realize that there is only this!

Without love or peace there is pain and suffering and a perceived sense of separation from the White Light of Source. It is this sense of separation that is created by ego thus self absorption, which then produces a desire of entitlement. Thoughts are then fear based as ego argues for its existence either through having everything or undeserving of nothing. So then the cycle of despair begins. What this means is that in order to feel a sense of entitlement one thinks that one must first experience pain, suffering, revenge or discomfort. This view then translates into, where is my ease in life or I deserve more or something better.

In other words, *I am entitled to this because of my suffering and all that I have gone through,* which is the core feeling of undeserving and feeling pain and living as a victim. So believing that you are undeserved, unworthy, and filled with no self-esteem, may be due to an experience in your life, whether it is present or past childhood trauma. What happens then is the following: you go to therapy to work through your feelings of undeserving, unworthiness, low self-esteem, and more. However, what has occurred here is some therapeutic interventions have placed and replaced one pain with another pain or suffering. Some therapists have moved you from pain of unworthiness to feeling that you deserve everything in life because the universe *owes you!* This is the same kind of pain and suffering wrapped around the feelings of undeserved or unworthiness. It is the same thing!

Don't you see? What now do you say? "Here I am after many years of therapy and now feeling strong, deserving, worthy, confident, and more, but now this is wrong?" No, this not what is being said. The strength, empowerment and the openness of you being the vessel or instrument for Spirit to move through you is within the absence of pain and feeling that you are lacking something. When you believe that you deserve something, you are still believing in pain of not enough. "I deserve everything because of what happened to me as a child." This view is no longer relevant with the new energies that are emerging from Spirit.

One needs to let go of anything that is making you feel entitled to anything. Because if you feel entitled, then you are still feeling empty. When you reach a state in life where you understand and feel that entitlement or deserving is simply self–absorption, then you will be fully in alignment with being awakened.

Your job here on the planet is to live through love and to share the love and that is it – wrapped of course around this love is peace, bliss, joy, and stillness. This is the only soul's purpose or soul's journey you need. This requires that you believe and feel that you are not entitled to anything. You see, if you feel that you deserve everything then you attract more deserving or pain because you feel you do not have what you need. So this emptiness of *not having* will continue to occur. To turn this around one needs to say, "I am complete and whole and whatever happens in my life will happen – I know, feel, believe, and allow abundance to flow into my life with the wave of the energy. I believe, know, and allow all messages from Spirit to move through me. I am open. I am an instrument of peace and I feel this is to be true."

As you shift along with the original world, you will become more familiar with these three terms: entitlement, deserving, and undeserving (see glossary on next page). All are the same – all hold the thoughts and the energies of pain, not enough and suffering. When awakened to your enlightenment stance of being, you then realize that you are enough. You are entitled and deserve to be who you truly are – one of love and peace. That's it!

If you feel you are deserving to be your authentic self, this then means you are not your authentic self, which indicates you have not awakened to the fact that you are already love and peace. In fact, the energy and Spirit of love and peace deserve and are entitled to *shine* through you. This is the *spiritual deserving* which is the true deserving. This deserving is the pure and core feeling of Spirit and it is now time to push deserving through the human form. Spirit will provide Divine interventions or synchronicities in order for the human to awaken to his/her true self and to no longer feel deserving, entitled, or undeserving.

Therefore, the deliverance of this deserving is through Spirit, for Spirit to deliver itself through form. Spirit deserves and is entitled to create modalities and/or causes (meaning causes in creation) in order for the human to realize who he/she really is (see glossary on next page for definition of modalities). You may have experienced this in your own life. Perhaps a sudden awakening or realization or perhaps an inner knowing pulls itself forward, or as some may call a crisis occurs to create an awakening. When this occurs, this creates an awareness like you have never experienced before. You then arrive in such a place of renewal that you will wonder why didn't this happen to me before. This place allows you to move into a great peace, a great stillness and the existence of now. The next movement is to a higher vibrational existence and this is Love of the deepest kind.

This Love is you, is God, is Spirit! You are this. In fact, you are simply all encompassing of all goodness to the highest degree. So much so that all plans, ideas, thoughts, and feelings resonate only from love. This true form of Love is the purest you can ever imagine and all things stem from Love. It is in this place where you exist, that place of the solidity of stillness or peace.

Glossary
1. Entitlement – not enough or I feel that I am owed. Perhaps you aren't owed anything and that the owing simply means "not enough."
2. Deserve – not enough and I am owed.
3. Undeserving – not enough.
4. Modalitites – the action or the spiritual creation of causes or incidences that bring you closer to Spirit through Divine interventions.

Yes to Life

This Crystal Collective All Truth is one that will prepare you for the "resonation of all things." The dictionary definition of resonation is "the natural frequency is the same as the frequency of the source." In other words, it is the harmonization of all White Light beings and Source to the same vibration or frequency. When you have awakened yourself, you have then placed yourself within the energy of resonating for and to the highest good of all things. You become equipped with passion, compassion, peace, joy, love, and bliss. When you begin to feel this resonation with all beings or the Oneness, you begin to feel what is required in order to serve and thus receive. What occurs naturally when awakened is you begin to serve and you begin to say:

Yes to life, yes to serving,
Yes to the alive awakened state,
Yes to you, yes to allowing,
Yes to believing, yes to knowing,
Yes to receiving, yes to giving,
Yes to the fine point of balance.

This fine point of balance is when one declares yes to serving and yes to allow receiving for oneself; yes to allowing a balance of both. When awakened, this feeling of balance occurs naturally and you begin to feel and know how this is achieved.

When in balance, you not only give your love of self to all but also allow the receiving of love for yourself. If you are a person who serves all the time and believes that there is no time for yourself, read this next part very carefully!

When living in an awakened state you just know when to say yes. You know that, no matter what, you are always filled with love because that is who you are – *love*! No matter what, your love will not dry up or be extended too much. This is an old ego saying, "Don't give so much because there will be nothing left over for you." Now some of this is true if you are unawakened, but if you are awakened you will know exactly what is being explained here. Yes means, "Yes, how can I help?" and then when you say this and the help is coming from you as the vessel or instrument of peace as messaged or played by Spirit, how could you not replenish? In fact, replenishing is never an issue because you are Spirit and Spirit is you – One in the same – same in the One!

Yes, of course you need to rest, sleep, dance, spin, twirl, sing, play, eat wonderful foods, and laugh. All of these are saying, "Yes, how may I serve through my laughter and playing in the sand?" This serving of play and laughter may be others watching you and feeling the energy or vibration you are resonating from the laughter and playing. Thus you are still serving within your rest and play. No matter what, you are serving and receiving and you resonate with everyone and everything – all beings, all of life. Even just a smile will be serving somebody and then allow *you* to receive the giving of that person's smile. Thus the reception of the energy from *smile*.

Suppose you say yes to serve, but when unawakened you expect something in return, perhaps money or at least something? However, when awakened you enter a state of existence where you don't need to receive something because you feel and understand that if nothing in material form is given then you still feel the act – the spiritual act of serving! That is all! This is how Mother Teresa lived her life upon the planet. You just live a life resonating with all beings. You are One with all. By serving others, you are serving yourself not in an ego-based way but in a way of spiritual connectedness. Observe how this circle of Oneness works, see below:

All beings are One. All are within this circle called *isness*. This isness of all beings is the thread that creates the Oneness of the circle. It is here within the circle that each being exists in beauty and harmony with oneself.

isness

When one lives from the isness of self then one is authentic, true, and genuinely filled with peace, stillness, bliss, love, grace, passion, and compassion. When *isness* exists, you are serving others just by being your authentic self and nothing more. You just say yes to you, to Divine Love.

The isness includes plants and animals as well, not just the *isness* of human beings but other beings as well. This isness is centered within the circle of Oneness. The center is the greatness of your authentic self. It is here within this *isness* where all beings connect as One. The authentic/isness of plants and animals is always there; nothing distorts itself from being authentic or isness. Plants and animals are always encircled with isness and when you, as the human being, became the isness you then become the One of the Oneness of nature. When walking in the forest, you resonate highly with the forest because you are the Oneness. You are your isness much like the forest. You may feel at home when in the forest because when awakened you then become aware to your resonation with nature and all beings/ creatures.

This is exciting and wonderfully brilliant in all the spiritual feelings of love, bliss, peace, stillness, grace, passion, and compassion.

Love Glue

Within each of the Crystal Collectives is the All Truths message concerning a "cohesive glue." The glue is the Source/God/White Light. This glue or Source has been holding everything together and is now strengthening its bond as now it is suggesting that this is a time to glue yourself to the Oneness within yourself and to others. As well the glue or the Spirit is coming forth at a pace that is considered to be in perfect timing for all and has been holding the planet together for millions of years. This is the adhesiveness of the cohesiveness. In order to be cohesive or clear of Spirit, one needs to be adhesive to Spirit, and recognize the glue is becoming stronger. It is tightening its hold and intensifying its message and increasing awakenings within all people.

The Spirit is tightening its love grip glue or adhesiveness in order for a cohesiveness or Oneness to occur! This is it. This *cohesiveness* is the Oneness and is the isness of the Oneness. As one person awakens to the state of peace, of stillness, of love, then another will follow and so on and so forth. All people will one day be awakened to the realization of who they truly are. It is a most amazing time in history. So, simply stated, allow the adhesiveness of Spirit to move through you in order for the cohesiveness to occur or the Oneness of all beings.

Karma

This next All Truth scribed within the catacombs of the Crystal Collectives is the term "karma" which means the way of existing. The law of attraction is woven into this existence. Karma, *that which is created by you,* is the energy that you create. It is the energy flow or the fluidity of the law of attraction and the way in which one moves and shifts through life, it is something you create. If you are a person who has created a life built upon fear, anger, worry, or frustration, then this will surely come back to you because the law of attraction or universe believes that this is what you are asking for – more anger, fear, worry, and frustration. You are now living in a time when karma appears to be immediate and instant. If, for example, you live in a place that is peace-filled, love filled, gentle, blissful, and compassionate, then this is your karma and this is what you will attract back to you immediately.

Karma is your expression of feelings, thoughts, ideas, judgments, opinions, responses, and reactions. Do you wish your karma to be of lower vibration or of higher vibration? Which do you want to put out in the world? Which do you want to have come back to you? You decide – this is called free will or choice and you experience the consequences of your choices. The term *consequences* means attractions and not punishment. Attraction – nothing more and nothing less. It is the way of the universe or Spirit.

As the world evolves spiritually into the original, so are you and all people. In fact, as stated earlier, the ego is being cleared and cleansed. The ego is the toxic karma, which is defined as lower vibration, anger, fear, suffering, and frustration. You may wish to live your life filled with positive karma emitting from you which resonates truly who you are, one of love, joy, peace, passion, and compassion. The karma of the energy of this way of being is of higher vibration and one of greatness in the White Light of love.

As you live in 2012 and onward in years, your patterns of behaviors will become refined and contained. Which means your behavior patterns will shift and be exposed more readily – this is the working of karma. The life you are presently living is one where you experience karma one millisecond by one millisecond or longer. It doesn't matter, but what does matter from Source/the White Light of love within you is the way in which you conduct yourself. You are the conductor of the orchestra of your life. If you so choose to conduct your orchestra with low vibrational music, then you will attract an audience to listen to and participate and even create more of the same type of low vibrational music.

You are the conductor – nobody else is but you! Therefore watch how you conduct your life! Do you feel the need to conduct your life orchestra with high vibrational or low vibrational music? The results of attraction of your karma is almost immediate, it is now! In these times of great shifts and changes, lessons are learned faster than ever before.

When living as you live, live fully and deeply from this place of high vibration of stillness, peace, bliss, passion, and compassion. This is the only place to be because this is who you really are: an instrument of peace. An instrument that is actually being played through you by Source. Remember you conduct the instrument or the orchestra by sleeping well, eating properly, relaxing, and resting. You need to clean and take care of your vessel (human form). As more humans awaken to who they are, they become more open for all things to happen for them. They begin to move and shift through life differently. For example, if you are a musician or an artist and have been awakened, you may then begin to create, design, and then perform or implement music that is of a higher vibration. Music that will entice higher conscious existence within all beings and this means music with spiritual meaning, tone, voices, sounds, and quiet space. These forms of music are now beginning to reveal themselves for all to hear. Listen and feel tenderly these pieces of music because *you* are the instrument being played by Source. You are conducting the instrument and also taking care of it! Be peace! Be still!

Senses

This message is indicating that your senses will be changing. They will become more attuned or sensitive. They will begin to open up and be lively and engaging. You will notice that when you are in nature you will deeply feel and hear its message from a high sensory point of view.

You may even wish to sit on the belly of Mother Earth or on a bench – whatever will best work for you and when in a most still or comfortable position, allow yourself to close your eyes and hear nature and then sense its energies. Feel the warmth and the flow emanating from the belly of Mother Earth move up into your solar plexus (abdominal area). Feel her softness and her nurturing. Then place your arms upward, pointing toward the sky, and feel the warmth of the Father Sky and Source flooding down upon you. Visualize a bright Light from Source flood down your entire form. Then stay here within this warmth from the Mother and the Father. Sense and feel these two energy forces and how they connect within you.

The All Truth message is that "all beings will be able to sense both of these energies as a very powerful and intense feeling as one moves through 2012 and post. When you are awakened, so does your whole sensory system. You awaken the nervous system of touch, feel, hear, taste, and smell – all of these senses become alive and aware. They become engulfed with glee, bliss, and gratitude and you begin to sense the subtleties of Spirit and its energies. You begin to sense a new way of being on a whole new level of what you experienced or knew about before."

When not awakened, you are living a life in a sleep state. Perhaps you would even go for a walk in the woods or garden and not be aware of the many butterflies flittering from one flower to the next or the fireflies flickering in the night space. Or see the tiny vein in the shimmering grass pointing toward Father Sky in order to replenish itself in its little life suit of green. But now, once awakened, you will notice all of this. Everything in nature will pop out for and to you. You will be amazed at how you see and feel color differently, how you touch and taste everything in life differently. You will even be able to hear more clearly. These senses become fully engaged and alive. Be prepared because this will happen and you will become attuned to the Spirit world as well.

As the veil between form and Spirit thins, you as a human will have access to the Spirit more readily. Living in 2012 and post 2012, the veil thins and during these times you will be able to draw upon other White Light Spirits to provide messages to and for you. It will become a way of living for you – how exciting this is!

The All Truth within this Crystal Collective also states that "not only will your sensory system become fully alive and engulfed in Spirit and energy, but will also assist in raising your energy vibration, and ensuring that you remain on the golden path of maintaining great health. In addition, the energy bodies or the chakras within each human will be changing not only color but their rotational directions will also change."

The seven energy bodies (the seven chakras) within the forms of the human will be shifting as the planet's energy vibration or energy body shifts. What you will find is that each color of the chakra will dissolve into white – a purity of white. This is the Homo-Luminous body color – white, which is all of the colors streamed together. The colors of the rainbow attached to the chakras will no longer be valid.

In fact there will be several more chakras attached to the Homo-Luminous body – as many as twelve to fourteen energy body layers and more. Do you see the pattern here? All symbols, signs, representations, knowledge, wisdom, studies, resources, and more of these solid low vibrational forms are all falling away, disappearing, leaving only the Homo-Luminous body in a world that has risen its vibration for all to live through and within its glory.

When one studies the present-day chakras, especially those working as practitioners of energy work, body talk, Reiki, and more, keep in mind that all of the numbers, colors, and representations of the chakras will be dismantled and dissolved energetically on each human. This takes place as he/she awakens to only the purity of White Light. It is within this White Light where the human Spirit form exists. It will be fascinating for those of you who work in this field of energy body work to begin to feel the shift of the White Light of Love moving into and through the human. Thus shifting, clearing, and cleansing blockages instantly. You will no longer need to slowly move into the perceived difficulties, you just need to allow. Do the following: when a client arrives for a treatment/session, talk with him/her gently and then lay your hands upon either his/her solar plexus or heart and allow the White Light of Love to move through you to him/her. You will also feel the White Light of Love moving from him/her to you and this exchange will be an amazing experience. Allow this White Light to do all the work now. You simply step back. Enjoy the White Light of Love moving through your sensory self. This is the work of love. Just allow what needs to happen, happen.

Nature and the Suns

This next discussion deals with nature once again because within the All Truths are the core pieces of what will occur to and for Mother Earth and Father Sky. During 2012 and post-2012 both Mother Earth and Father Sky will be cleaning and cleansing themselves in order to create anew. As they are cleansing and cleaning, they are also rejuvenating themselves. When humans begin to awaken to who they really are, which is One with Spirit, and as this vibration increases, it clearly affects the planet. But until more people become awakened, the Mother and the Father need to cleanse and communicate this in order for people to realize that the Mother and the Father need help. Some may call this tough love, but it is only the communication of love or a reminder to love. This may take the form of heavy rains, droughts, and the extinction of certain animals and plants until the Mother and Father are heard and felt. This is not intended to create any form of fear or threat but only for awareness and observing what is occurring upon the planet. Remember that everything is in perfection. Everything is shifting and transforming and renewing all back to Spirit. *All* is good.

As more people awaken, then the planet, Mother Earth, and Father Sky will be able to increase their vibration. What this actually entails is the following: the sun, moon, stars, comets, and more will shift in shape and even form. The stars may even seem brighter and in different locations. The sun becomes a fuller white in color (depicting all colors). The moon will begin to take shape differently and even the Milky Way will evolve into a different form of beauty. The weather patterns will begin to take on a different form and become more temperate and not as harsh. There will even be new ideas and ways to create paper-made products or wood products instead of cutting down trees. In other words, Mother Earth will be respected instead of being used irresponsibly.

The atmosphere will also clear and rejuvenate as the energy vibration increases. In addition, as the atmosphere changes and clears, it also releases toxic fumes, and negative energies which will immediately be met by White, Loving, Transformative Light. This means that the fullness of Life emerges – its healing qualities, its vastness, its way of just being, its isness. The way it holds everything together – it just is – there are no words to describe its isness because isness has no language to explain itself.

Also realize that as Mother Earth, Father Sky, and the atmosphere shift and change, so do the inner nature details within it change. In other words the increased vibration creates an increased vibration within the Mother's belly of soil, which then will increase the vibration of all plants and of course animals (including humans) because they eat the plants and for some, the animals. The plants will increase the vibration within the animal that feeds upon it. So you see, as you increase your vibration, so does the planet and the circle continues because the planet, Mother Earth, Father Sky, and atmosphere will then feed and give back to you what you are giving it. Thus the law of attraction – the food will be nourishing, the atmosphere temperate, the sun of beautiful heat, the oceans have calmed as have the skies, the rainbows have relaxed into different shapes and forms, and more! Reader, this does sound very futuristic and surreal but feel and think this one through: as the vibration increases upon the planet then the beauty of this vibration will influence the planet and the universe in a most incredible, renewing way. These times are truly exciting.

If you, as the human continue to provide low vibrational energies to the planet, the Mother and the Father will need to continue to clear and cleanse themselves from the toxins as created by the humans. Try to imagine this most beautiful, perfect world filled with all that was described previously with high vibrational qualities and quantities. Thus the recreation of the Garden of Eden.

One of beauty and design. One of great
joy and a gladness of being.
One of substantial energy and Spirit. One of great tidings!
This is the original world – the way of existing.

With such high vibration upon the planet you will notice that even the cloud formations will shift and change as the atmosphere and weather change. Clouds will form differently and will take on several forms of light – not just blue and white. They will be most spectacular. Also become very familiar with the sun for the sun has many messages for you to pay attention to. In fact, the sun is not the only sun that will make its appearance; other suns will also come forward for the humans to feel and acknowledge. These suns are suns of the Source, meaning feelings that are connected to the sun will shine forth and are feelings that will communicate to you. These feelings will communicate through you simply by you accepting what they have to offer. These suns will be within the sky energetically and will then very slowly appear to the naked eye over the next many years. These little suns will need to make themselves known post-2012 because of feelings they wish to share. These feelings are ones that will speak about the next stages of the spiritual evolution, which are the transitional and metamorphosis stages. These two stages are the next two stages post-2012. Within these suns, one will discover the following and more:

1. A deeper feeling of Spirit.
2. A deeper connection to nature.
3. A deep, stronger, and higher vibration of energy.

Try sitting quietly with the sun as you see and feel it now today, and in the early morning with the sunrise or evening with the sunset. You see, these two specific times are times that are best served to listen and feel the sun.

Also included within the above shifts in nature are the elements of fire (sun), water, air, earth, and ether. The water is just as important as the trees and the earth equally as important as the bright, shining stars. Elements also mean origin; originating from earth are plants, from water growth and food, from fire rejuvenation, from air breath, and from ether Spirit. These elements will be changing their forms and shapes to the point where they will no longer need to be labeled and/or recognized because the only form of element will be the Spirit within all forms. The term *elements* will no longer need to be used or implemented because it implies separation or specialness.

The original world becomes the *origin,* meaning that everything is original or One with origin. There is no need for any symbolic representation of any element due to the fact that all beings and nature are connected to Source – meaning Oneness. Therefore this leads to the Crystal Collective of All Truths that states, "All beings have plan and purpose of soul, which is love." There is no hierarchy anymore – all will be resonating on the same plane. All beings are created equal in Spirit. All are the same – no need to separate or define difference.

You will also notice that the study of shamanism will also begin to shift as shamans too release their hierarchy of animal Spirits. Their ways to honor Spirit will also change. You will not only see the releasing of symbols, patterns, and programmings within shamanism but also within other ceremonies of White Light. A whole new beginning or just a realization or awakening to what is? Thus coordinating with the Oneness or an empty vessel filled with Spirit.

The First Nations people are also beginning to shift and reshift their way of honoring Spirit. Some of these peoples already know and have been listening and feeling Mother Earth and Father Sky for several years now and have already begun to make this shift. They have the inner ability to connect to not only sun of the Father and the soil of the Mother but also the thunder, the clouds, and the little plant Spirits. They already have been preparing for this shift and just know instinctively what is occurring.

As you can see, the Spirit of greatness or "the Great Spirit," as known by the First Nations peoples, is remolding the Earth with its hands upon the flexible clay of the world. The flexibility of the clay depends upon the vibration the planet receives from the human's vibration. Higher vibrational energy creates more flexibility than the harsh low vibrational energy. A higher vibrational energy is warmer, more loving and still, than a lower vibrational energy, therefore leading to a softer, more pliable or flowing way of existing.

This flowing way of existing reflects the fluidity of how humans will live when in the flow of emotion and Spirit. This is reflected as increased vibrational energy, increased flexibility, increased warmth of the feeling of peace, stillness, love, and therefore increased fluidity and flow of Life. Everything reflects everything around it and mirrors Spirit and the perfection of Oneness.

Equality

As we move through 2012 and post-2012, you will see the birthing of equality of all races, sexes, ages, names, colors, languages, and sexual orientations. Within the Crystal Collectives of the All Truths, the issue of inequality will no longer be an issue. "What you are presently now seeing is a spiritual evolution of the concept equality on a grand scale. This issue of inequality will no longer exist and will easily dissolve into the mist of transformation." Certainly, there will be a process to follow, but it also depends upon the vibration of the planet. When the planet vibrates at a high rate of energy, then issues such as these dissolve with an easiness that then creates a new way of being for all people.

The more awakened people become, the more likely they will stop believing in the inequality of all people. *Open arms of acceptance* are extremely important during these fantastic times of change. It remains vital that when you catch yourself thinking, feeling, or making a racial statement that you immediately stop. Or if you hear or feel someone is also doing the same then you need to say something. Begin today to shift into a new way of being. Now is the time to begin this shift and awaken.

Receiving Love and Giving Love = Abundance

This next All Truth deals with the "inner existence of Spirit itself." What this means is that, as more people awaken and allow themselves to be a vessel for Spirit to move through them, then the Spirit actually makes itself known more strongly or in a higher and more intense energy or vibration because, and only because, you are saying, "Yes, I am accepting. Yes, I am believing and allowing and now receiving." What the Spirit does in an energetic format is similar to jumping up and down and cheering. It makes itself known in all ways in your life – not just one form but in others. This is how the law of attraction works. More goodness will come your way when you fully engage and awaken to Spirit – this being you. You are God, White Light of Love, and Source.

The Source will then stream its high vibrational energy through you and this process begins slowly right at that point of feeling awakened. Sometimes this streaming of energy is so intense it can become overwhelming, as stated in earlier messaged chapters. So just relax, get grounded with lots of rest, and eat properly. But what this message from the All Truth is saying is that more comes your way when you are awakened. When you awaken further, more love energy is imprinted within you and as more love comes to you the circle repeats and then more awakenings occur. It really is this simple. Just remember that, when you begin to awaken, a slow force of love energy will come your direction in the most beautiful ways! The key or the most important part of all of this is for you to accept the feeling of love and all that it attracts for you.

This is also known as *abundance*. Abundance is available to all people – not just to those who feel they are awakened. How does abundance take its form from what was just described? It's a simple approach: when one begins to realize that love – Spirit of love or its energy of love – is within oneself and has much to offer not only within oneself but to others as well then more love will come to that person. If you radiate love, more will come to you. As stated earlier, it is as if Spirit jumps up and down and cheers, "Yahoo!" When this energetic connection is made with the Spirit of love, then watch what happens and feel what happens. Taste, touch, and even smell what happens. More love comes your way – accept it! When the abundance energy is allowed to flow, the Spirit literally sings, "Hallelujah!" just for you. This energy of abundance will flow in many forms, such as more love, passion, bliss, compassion, job opportunities, and relationships. The beginning or the start of this flow of abundance needs to begin with love and only love.

When love is available, then everything else will flow from this. The abundance then grows and grows and the more you accept, the more is gifted. It literally is the universe or Spirit saying, "Okay, we will give you more because you are in love and accepting" and then more arrives.

Just allow the abundance to come your way, believe it is here, and know more is arriving because the abundance within Spirit is endless! There is so much abundance for each person that you can't even calculate it. This sounds so unbelievable, but believe it to be true and just allow love to flow through you, for you, to others.

Vibrations within Countries

The All Truth within this Crystal Collective is communicating that "the energies, themselves, are shifting vibrationally within themselves." In other words, the core of the energy pattern shifts as humans shift their energy. To clarify, the energetic result of a spiritual awakening or realization is so incredibly powerful vibrationally, that not everybody in the entire world needs to be awakened fully to see and feel the shift upon the planet. This shift is felt by all naturally and will be recognized by all.

In fact, even if one person experiences a *point of feeling the awakened state* but doesn't fully recognize it or understand the feeling and then dismisses it, even the millisecond point of an awakened feeling creates an amazing high-frequency vibration. This will add to the planet's vibration in a very powerful manner. This may occur to those who are living in countries where there is extreme physical poverty, abuse, torture, and war. However these people may at some point in their life experience this point of the feeling of awakening, and this becomes extremely important because this point of being awakened for even one second or less will increase that country's vibration. Just one second or millisecond from one person will assist in the country's awakened state. There may be fewer people within a particular country living these points of awakening, however this does not mean that they cannot be raised energetically vibrationally. One persons' point of awakening is everyone else's as well.

What this in fact does mean is for other developed countries to awaken themselves in order to shift the lower vibration of these countries. A developing country is exactly that – a country evolving or developing in all ways and it is important for a country such as this to develop its awareness at some level of the law of attraction.

You see, what else would these people know except for poverty, fear, worry, disease, rape, war, and torture? And if they believe these will continue, then the universe will give the country more of the same – as written in the All Truths. How is this really different from a developed country focused upon greed, ego, hatred, encouragement of war (which is killing people), fear, and continued abuse? You see, one person at a time is being awakened and his/her energy vibration will assist the planet's energetic vibration immensely – not all people of the world need to shift, just a certain percentage.

Again, realize that the core of energy vibrates so incredibly high that, as stated, just one person feeling a millisecond point of awakening will shift the vibration of the planet and, in particular if he/she is living in a developing country situation, then this energy vibration will be felt immensely within his/her own country.

The White Light when turned on dissolves the darkness! This is an all-time, forever, and ever All Truth or mystic law permanently etched into the Crystal Collectives of each and every collective.

Be aware then that, as we move through 2012 and beyond you will feel the impact of the high vibrational energy force from Spirit. The core of this is love's design and creation, which is whole and complete; Love at its best! This feeling of love within is the energy of Spirit. This feeling within the core is the energetic vibration of love that can heal or some would say cleanse, clear, and rejuvenate. Miracles and blessings occur through love! This is another eternal All Truth.

Desire

This next Crystal Collective message within the All Truth is the collective of messages concerning "desiring" and it is here within the difference between desiring where your *desire for that which you believe you don't have* rather than the *desire of who you are*, is explained.

The desire to know who you are simply means awakening to your desire of a spiritual being within a human form. This first desire is one of love. *I desire to love myself and I desire to awaken to this state of being – of who I really am! Now is the time.* So you create the desire and wait in readiness for your point of awakening.

The second desire could be explained through the example of addiction. Perhaps you have been living a life of drug addiction, which presented you the illusion of filling up that empty space but this just didn't seem to work. So then you desire more intense drugs to feel better and still this does not work. You then realize the drugs do not fulfill your desire to feel good. So now you may say, "I desire to feel love, the core of existing." This means, "I am ready. It is my time, my turn." This desire is one where you desire to be somebody different because you are unhappy with who you are believing yourself to be. You desire to know, feel, and realize that bliss, joy, and love are available because you are Spirit.

You see these desire differences? One desires suffering as a victim lost and unable to understand and feel that which you keep is already within you. You just need to tap into this part of you. If you don't know this, then this desiring holds the answer for you in purchasing material goods, moving away, frequent shallow relationships, addiction, unstable jobs, and style of living.

Realize that within this *just be-ing* is your Crystal Collective of messages and All Truths. What this means is that once you feel this desire to know who you are – your Spirit, your Oneness with all and Source – you then *begin* and you meet that still point of awakening because desire is the beginning of the transition of the *movement to the still point*. This is the point at which you allow yourself to become awakened to the realization of who you are. So stop desiring that which is outside yourself. Look at your inner desire in order to move into who you already are, which is Spirit in human form.

"I desire to feel the core of my existence.
I desire to feel my spiritual way of
being. I desire to assist others.
I desire to allow, know, and believe that I am Spirit,"
and through this desire or, in other words, saying,
"I am ready; it is my time/my turn."
You then change your life.

But if you turn your desire into the desiring of suffering again then the energy or vibration of this desire begins to emerge, thus creating and manifesting more desiring and a return to more intense drugs for the one who is drug addicted and therefore a relapse. This then becomes an extremely sad situation because you are not seeing that which is inside of you as Spirit. This *isness* is Spirit. This is who you are: a being of beauty, love, peace, joy, and compassion for self and others.

Often when humans are placed or place themselves into a perceived suffering or crisis situation, this is the point where they begin to rethink and feel life all over again. At this point, they have the ability to move into their true whole desire of *who am I, and I am ready to know, feel, believe, and allow all to come forward. It is my time now!* When a human states this, then he or she is ready and willing for the awakening to occur.

This ends this message through the Crystal Collectives regarding desire. As stated earlier, these Crystal Collectives are within you. These messages are within you.

Indulge in Your Being of Self

This next Crystal Collective All Truth will message to you all about life and what this life really means when living through the state of just "being." This state of being is of Oneness with self and Oneness with who you really are. This information has already been covered several times in this book, but this discussion is more detailed and more about being One with self and being self-indulgent with self. This does not mean you are self-centered, selfish, or being self-absorbed but to indulge in your self – your Spirit, your Soul, your *who you really are.*

Sit quietly and visualize the following. You are walking along the beach with ten friends and you begin to notice that one friend at a time leaves the walk to go home until finally you are the only one walking along the beach. Now it is sunset. You have encountered one of the most amazing energetic times through the day, a sunset. You are peace-filled, complete without others, complete with self, knowing you are not alone, and believing that each millisecond you live through is in perfection. Allowing each millisecond to be noticed, loving each millisecond of the present now and feeling loved by the friends who have retired to their families or others. The high energy vibration that they gave you leaves you feeling beautiful because you also gave them love, peace, and joy. This above visualization is indulging in self, feeling and experiencing it in every spiritual moment of your life, being present in *the everything*, every feeling, all parts and pieces of life at that moment! Self-indulgence means experiencing life in Spirit, self, Source/God – all of this and more.

Indulging in suffering, pain, fear, materiality, self-pity, selfishness is considered self-absorption or self-indulgence of another kind. Which displays itself as self-dislike, fear, and abandonment of your trueness of self. The difference here is for you to feel okay and good and that when feeling the self-indulgence of connecting to Spirit you are then awakening to your true self. So when you walk the beach alone, indulge in being aware of everything and every feeling that is occurring around and through you. Recognize this as self-care of Spirit – of who you are.

Yes, you are a Spirit in human form and a form with Spirit. For some, you are a Spirit trying to understand how to live in a human body life or a human body life understanding how to live a spiritual life. Which are you? A Spirit living a human life or a human living a spiritual life? Both are similar but yet dissimilar.

If, for example, you are selectively living grounded in your form and materiality, but have not yet connected to your spiritual existence, then you are form trying to live a spiritual existence. If you are ungrounded by living mainly through Spirit, then you are Spirit trying to live through the human form. Both of these existences are in essence the same, however you need the balance between the two. You need to awaken to your Spirit while living the human form of existence and now live as Spirit grounded in human form, all in balance. Thus self-indulgence, indulging in one's own self-awareness of Spirit and one's own self-awareness of body. To be grounded in Spirit means you are then balanced and able to serve as Spirit moves through you in a most beautiful fashion, self-indulging within your self-care within Spirit. Indulge in Spirit and awaken to who you are, Spirit moving through the form – the deeply grounded balanced form. That is all.

So walk along the beach and realize that everything is being gifted to you. Accept all gifts and it may just be hearing a bird's song or feeling the sand under your feet or the smell of the warm night air. And give grace and gratitude for all of these gifts because this gratitude and these graces are also indulgence. This means to indulge in thanksgiving, indulge in serving, indulge in silence, indulge in love, indulge in peace, and indulge in joy. As you indulge, you self-care. As you self-care, you need to indulge. Indulgence therefore is the spiritual connection you acquire as you shift into the trueness of self. That is all!

Difference between Ego and Spirit

Now is the time to understand and to feel the difference between "ego and Spirit" as described within the All Truths through this Crystal Collective. It is now the time to know what this means and feels like when ego is speaking and when the grace of Spirit is speaking. Grace is peace and stillness, a delicate way of existing. Ego which brings suffering, dismay, troubles, for some hatred, and for others self-sabotage.

Which will you choose? And choose consciously, being fully aware of the consequences of your choices, which include feelings, thoughts, ideas, opinions, and actions. If you decide to choose the White Light or grace, then you have decided to awaken yourself to who you really are and in fact ready to unfold in life. You are then ready to live an awakened life. If, however, you choose a life of ego suffering – believing everything the ego states or dictates to you which is unreal and illusion, then life will be difficult and not as fulfilling as that of Spirit/White Light. So again here are your two choices:

Suffering and following your ego of not being worthy,
being filled with fear and pain, and self-sabotage.
or
Not suffering, but following Spirit of love, peace, joy,
and simplicity and asking how may I serve?

If one believes ego, suffering or darkness, one then becomes so engaged in suffering and pain that he/she will eventually decide, "Enough pain, enough suffering, I can't do this anymore." When this occurs, then one is able to see *the Light at the end of the tunnel.* The tunnel is their pain and suffering and the Light is their true awakened self of Spirit and Light. Some people may need to shift or live in the darkness of ego suffering in order to feel the White Light and then to help others shift out of their own darkness.

Therefore your soul's contract may be intermingled with all of this as well. Perhaps you signed up to live within the ego state or the darkness in order to experience this so that you could help others escape and free themselves and become awakened. Oftentimes, the human will move out of his/her dark places into the Light, which may occur through a suffering or a crisis situation. This is most common.

Sometimes humans believe that one is able to move more deeply into one's soul, one's Spirit, when in a crisis. This may be true for some. However, you actually can move faster into Spirit or the awakened state when living in a state of love and trusting. When living from this place, one then begins to feel, know, believe, and trust life. If a perceived crisis or trauma (divorce, death, or loss of job) happens, then you will know, believe, and allow that the reason for this resides within the beauty of all things occurring for Divine purpose and reason.

Perhaps the Divine or your intuition has been speaking to you and you did not trust its voice. Therefore the voice needed to get louder and the Divine needed to place you in a position where you were forced to listen.

How the law of attraction works with this is quite simple. If you are within a relationship that is filled with lies from your partner but you don't want to hear the lies, then the universe or Spirit will give you more of this because this is what you are asking for. This is what you are attracting ("I can't hear these lies; I can't trust myself"). So the universe will present situations exactly like this. Not trusting yourself and not being able to hear the lies but creating untruths and fantasies is ego and therefore you attract more *unrealities* into your world. When this begins to happen, you then create such an intense low vibration of energy that a crisis or a breaking point needs to happen. There is no choice energetically. This could be your discovery that your partner/husband/wife has been having an affair for several months and you knew this on all levels but continued believing the lies and the fantasies. When a situation like this occurs and you say, "I knew it!" this then is the breaking point for you!

This is now a time for you to move toward an awakened self, a life of trusting self and your intuition. Everything has been and is in perfect plan and order. No matter what! Some label the light as goodness or grace and ego as evil and darkness. Whatever terms you use, understand that all is on time, in perfect plan, reason and order. Everything is perfect!

Being aware that all is in perfect timing and order will always bring about great peace and stillness in situations. All situations are events, changes, and transitions meant to bring you closer to Spirit. Closer to an inner awakening or to that still point of decision to be awakened. All is perfect!

All Is Grand

This Crystal Collective is messaging to you through this All Truth that all is "grand and filled with beauty." All is filled with a flow of all of life. It is here within the arms of life you become One. When you begin to open more to possibility, you then change your aura to a clean, clear, White Light of Love, and you begin to also see other peoples' auras and energy systems. You begin to feel and see life differently. You become extremely sensitive to all things – all beings!

Therefore as you move closer to the realizations of self, you also become more aware of seeing auras, and sensing Spirits. The veil is thinning between form and Spirit, so you will become closer to being One with Spirit. You will be able to connect with Spirit at a visceral and real level. You will not only be able to see and read others' auras and your own aura but also the auras and the Spirits of nature. You will be able to hear and feel the wise old tales from the belly of Mother Earth. You will be able to taste the ocean's mist and feel its messages upon your tongue. You will be able to translate the songbird's beautifully filled tones of love. You will be able to hear the tiny footsteps of the baby chipmunk as it scurries across the belly of the Mother and feel its excitement to find its nurturance.

Instead of living a small life, you expand your form of existing and you become that which you are, all around you. You begin to see, feel, hear, taste, and touch all of life and not just one part of what life is. In other words, you will sense Spirits in nature and/or others. Perhaps you already see and sense auras. If you are able to do this already, then it will intensify and you will sense more. Life for you will become filled with more of life.

You will be able to sense so much more than this and even more than what you could possibly imagine. This is just the beginning! As you approach this time of the original world, you approach being One with Spirit. How exciting and beautiful this is!

Choose Peace

This Crystal Collective's message from the All Truths is "one can choose and live in peace if one wants to." This is your choice and nobody else's – your husband, wife, partner, children, friends, therapist, or doctor cannot decide for you! You decide. Do you choose peace or no peace? It is just this! If you choose peace, then everything you do, say, think, feel – everything – must be One of peace. Because of your choice, then the universe will say, "Here is more of this peace for you" because you attract more you then begin to change your life. New realizations occur and your awakened self springs forward. You see how this works?

The more you choose peace, the more peace will be gifted to you. In fact, when entering a forest you will immediately feel the peace emanating from the nature Spirits because you are now open for this to occur. When *open* in *peace*, which works in tandem because *peace* means that one is *open* to live a life filled with freedom and love. What this then means is that you may begin to open up pieces/peaces of yourself in order to acquire what you need in order to move into a most beautiful life. This is also called being *delicate*. It is a delicate, tender, careful way of being within yourself and with others. What peace does is it slows you down completely and rearranges your life in a most miraculous way. You decide automatically to relax and be still, to be filled with such grace that you begin to change thoughts, ideas, feelings, and opinions. You shift! It feels as if you live within a White Light blanket of stillness. It is large, soft and peacefully comforting. It has no special meaning or purpose except to accept, allow, know, and believe that you are peace. After all, that is who created you. The Source of peace – God or any name you give this One Source is so delicate and tender. It is so sweet, lovely, and soft. This is you! Yet it is empowering, powerful, and filled with strength and discernment.

When you live in this state of awakening, you will begin to experience a feeling of freedom and you may even notice a disease dissolve – this is very common. You are no longer living in *dis-ease* but with ease. Remember this is a choice – your choice. You may even begin to notice that you look younger; perhaps you no longer require reading glasses or any form of eyewear. Your mind, emotions, thoughts, all become still and clear. Your authentic self begins to shine forth and you remain in a place of *This is who I am. Nobody can tell me who I am anymore. It is my business or my choice to live from grace.*

Your leisure time changes its focus as well as all of your travels. The choice of living peace is the step into being awakened, which is the step into becoming and accepting the Homo-Luminous way of living. The rise of the awakening and living in peace and stillness is occurring at a rapid rate as more people are recognizing this way of being *as the only way of being.* Not only will you look and feel physically different but you will approach life differently. Softer, gentler, and in ease not *dis-ease.* Others will notice and feel this change and wonder what happened, and you can share this: "I have chosen peace."

Peace is the core of the Oneness of the original world – it is the stillness, it is the *isness* of all individual beings and as One, together. You may even discover that your physical form feels easier. Your physical form of skin, organs, cells, bones, and more all shift because your DNA is also shifting. Lots of sleep may not be necessary as you shift your energy(ies) vibrations to a higher level. You may feel that all of you is transitioning and metamorphosing into a most incredible being. This is truth!

Gentle Shifts

Wrapped within the arms of this next Crystal Collective is the All Truth of "protection, easement, assuredness, trusting, love, stillness, and joy for all people." When one is truly awakened, then these feelings become available to you because you are this already. You just begin to realize this. These Spirits or gems of the light will assist you through your awakenings as the planet shifts and changes.

As the vibrational patterns of energy increases, this energy's gentle shift will then tenderly move the tectonic plates and this will therefore create new ocean and land shapes or formations. The whole planet and universe are awakening to a newness – not just humans but the planet as a whole.

Everything is reshaping, reshifting, and reconstructing itself through the energetic changes or the spiritual changes from the awakenings through the human because of this everything will be refreshed and renewed. But do not fear: these shifts, shapes, and changes are occurring slowly and tenderly. The completion of the reshaping of the whole planet will be 3012, hundreds of years from December 21, 2012.

Even the DNA within the planet, plants, soil, animals, sea creatures, and humans will be shifting and changing for the better. As the human awakens to a higher vibrational frequency of energy, so too will his/her DNA, which will actually shift to twelve DNA components. (Read the next section in this book titled "The New DNA" for further details.) Once this is recognized emotionally, physically, and spiritually, then this too will affect and effect all of nature and therefore it too will change its DNA to match that of the human. This is truth! It is also evident that when the soil of Mother Earth raises her energetic vibration, changes her DNA pattern of cells, then food produced by her will also have a higher food quality, higher DNA component, and higher energetic vibration. The human then consumes the food or the animals eat the food and *voila,* wonderful energy replenishes the bodies. See how this most miraculous and profound energy cycle occurs when living through and within an awakened state? How beautiful this is! How wonderful this is!

The circle of the crystal world looks like a silver white circle, which depicts the energy cycle of what was just described. It is here within this energy cycle that the energy is streamed from soil to plant to animal, human, sea life, and back again and again. That is all! Within the beauty of this is the gentleness of all change. Some say it is a time of chaos and fear, this is not true. Simply embrace all shifts with love and know there is a grand reason and purpose. This is truth and this is scribed within the Crystal Collectives. It will take many years for the complete shift to occur, not just a couple of years; 2012 is just the beginning point for the shift and not the end point. The first most important point is the point of the feeling of being awakened. This is the most important point – nothing more than this!

The New DNA

With respect to the shifts of DNA, the number of DNA that humans will be receiving as they become awakened to their spiritual self is fourteen, and this is a *given*. These extra DNAs are connected to the Homo-Luminous body and will be regained when the human has metamorphosed into this deep state of awakening. These DNAs are attached to the human form in a different manner. It is a more spiritual/energetic connection that will allow the human to maintain its equilibrium while metamorphosing into the final White Light being that it is – the Homo-Luminous form or non-form! You may even request these fourteen DNA to rejoin your body, mind, Spirit, emotion and energy selves. Ask permission from these selves and allow three months or longer for the rejoining. The DNA rejoining feels as if a solidity or confidence of self has entered your wholeness. You feel stronger in all your selves of body, mind, Spirit, energy and emotion.

It is being shown through the All Truths within the Crystal Collectives that this full metamorphosis of the human into the Homo-Luminous body, along with the planet or universe will complete its evolution 3012. What this means is the circle or the new Mayan calendar then *expands* and finally disappears into the White Light of God/Source. Because the energy and Spirit of each being will be such that it matches the planet and the planet matches all humans who are now Homo-Luminous, therefore the planet is now Homo-Luminous, which is Spirit reigning the human form. Then all will slowly meld together as One pure White Light. All beings at this point in history will be melded together as One. No differences will exist within anything. All sexes, races, languages, and colors of skin will be melded as One entity, which is God Source/White Light. This is what the mystic laws or the All Truths are saying for this year of 3012. Nothing more, nothing less!

The illustrated book by Alex Grey entitled *Sacred Mirrors: The Visionary Art of Alexander Grey* has a vision of the Homo-Luminous body that is most accurate and incredible. It illustrates the melding of the form and Spirit together as One White Light. This is truth for all beings – to reach the highest awakened state possible which then melds you with the White Light of Source/God. This is called the state of being Homo-Luminous or the illuminated pure White Light form.

The above message from the All Truths may be required to be reread again. If you read this again feel the message – it is just simply stating that all people are shifting into a grand Oneness of White Light and this includes more DNA to assist in this process. How wonderful!

Surrender to Your Calling

A mong this Crystal Collective's All Truth are the pieces of messages that begin to pull the puzzle of life slowly together. These pieces of messages are always available to and for you. You just need to listen and feel them and know what they are when they arrive for you. These pieces of messages are the containers for you in order for you to solidify the knowing, believing, and allowing that are you! When you tap into these pieces of messages (crystal pieces), you truly become solidified in all that needs to be done.

The solidity or the strength of these pieces of messages as depicted in the crystals is the recognition and only the recognition that once you hear and feel these messages all will become clear for now! Life is geared and placed only in the *now!* Even if you are feeling called to do something in life, you need to live now! What can you do about this calling? Reach for the sky when being called. Say to Source, "I surrender and I am fully open to you. I am ready to move forward with my calling." These small pieces of crystal messages arrive slowly for you. They will begin to place people, signs, books, songs, angels in human forms, and more on your path to assist you moving forward with your calling. All is in plan and these crystal pieces or messages will flow into your life when you allow them. Know they are here or arriving and believe them when they arrive.

Trusting is most vital in this process. You may hear, feel, smell, taste, and touch a piece of message, but if you don't trust it then you may miss it. Trust your pieces of messages from Source. Allow and surrender to acceptance, and, when you do, more pieces of the crystal messages will arrive just for you! How wonderful and exciting! You see, your trust is so needed in this world now.

From now on is a time of reflection upon all of life. It is a time where all people will be faced with questions like these: "Who am I?" "What do I believe is truth and real?" "What is really going on here?" "What is my purpose in life?" "What is happening to the world and all people?" The energies and the Spirit are pushing and pulling forward in a large yet gentle way in order to tug people to see and feel their Spirit at a deeper and mature fashion. It is here where change occurs.

Listen and trust to what is transpiring here. Spirit is presenting to you a beautiful gift wrapped in silk for you to explore and enjoy. You determine if you would like to wear the gifts contained in the packages, all wrapped in silk, being Spirit wrapping paper and the gift being the fashion of love. This gift of love from Spirit is actually Spirit and is the most beautiful gift you could ever acquire in this lifetime. Accept it, wear it, and allow it to become you. You are the gift receiver, and thank the gift bearer which is Source/White Light. Accept this gift from Spirit and allow it to behold your nature – who you are. Allow it to become who you really, really are. This is the being who is needed for the original world; this White Light is *you*!

Jump into the Flow

This next Crystal Collective of the All Truths message gently implies that "all beings need to know that the planet is still slowly shifting, reshaping, and reshuffling no matter what." What this implies gently is that the thinning of the veil is occurring. The planet is physically, energetically, and spiritually shifting. People are being awakened as described, and what this means is that you just need to get onboard and flow with the high vibration of Spirit. You just need to shift into this awakened state of being, this place of stillness and peacefulness, this place of completeness. When you have awakened yourself to this state, which is always inside you because this is who you are, then you will be able to live from this *flow* of Spirit. This flow of the Divine. This flow of life and living from this love. Align everything with your flow of the Divine.

This flow is the Oneness, the line of eternity, the Crystal Collectives, the All Truths, the way of being in stillness and peace. This flow is truly who you are. It is your Essence that is the planet's Essence, which then means that you are the Divine.

As the planet moves naturally into the original world, so do you because you are the Divine. You will naturally slide into the still point of awakening and from there make a decision of being awakened or not. It is here at this still point where you decide to slide into a world of beauty, peacefulness, and stillness!

You are one of gentleness and Divinity of soul and Spirit. Jump into the flow, move, slide, and be swept away with the beauty of the planet as the veil thins and Homo-Luminous form approaches.

Depths of Your Being

This next Crystal Collective All Truth will message to you about the "depths of your being." The inner depths of who you are goes beyond what you even know or believe you are. You are deeper in Spirit than what you will ever comprehend, and there is no point in trying to understand this because there is no understanding or intellectualizing the Spirit. The Spirit lives and resonates on several different levels. These levels are complex and very simple, yet, there is no understanding of these levels. The Crystal Collectives All Truths say, "Just relax and stay in the moment and live from this moment and only from this moment as it is here where all of life exists."

In one single moment all of the levels of life exist.
It is here within this moment where Spirit is speaking.
Listen one moment by one moment.
Feel one moment by one moment.
Touch one moment by one moment.
You just need to arrive in the moment and
feel and be in that moment only.
Place all of your attention upon that moment.
Place all of you in that moment, that millisecond, because
that millisecond is perfectly planned especially for you!

The original world as it evolves will be allowing people to feel more about life and the depths of Spirit within themselves and outside themselves – moment by moment. The intricacies of Spirit go beyond any human understanding, any wisdom teachings as claimed by the human or any deep knowledge. Spirit is simply a feeling of Oneness.

Relax, be peace, be still, and enjoy this ride called *life* because that is what it is – a ride into Spirit. As these times approach for one to shift and evolve spiritually into the transparent form, one then begins to realize that Spirit is knowing. It is within the knowing you discover that there is no point in trying to figure everything out because you can't! There's more to life than what any human can understand. One can try to figure out reasons why things happen in life, but you may discover only a little tiny piece of *why* but not the truly inner spiritual reasons of *why!*

This message is clear! Relax and enjoy. Relax and become one with all that is of stillness, peace, and absolute love. Love each and every moment in your life right now and leave the reasons and figuring out for Spirit. Spirit's job is to assist you through one moment to the next moment, thus assisting you through everything that life offers you. Live and breathe through Spirit. It is here within Spirit where life reigns and is most powerful and empowered.

Source Increases Its Energetic Vibration

This section is messaged through the depths of the Crystal Collectives All Truth that indicates that "as people increase their vibration, then the energy/spiritual vibrations of the planet also increases and what occurs naturally is that the Source/White Light increases its vibration as well." Therefore as each human awakens to who he/she really is, this then increases his/her energetic vibration and begins to sense his/her intuition more openly. As one becomes accepting and following one's intuition, then more of these intuitive senses will arrive. What this incurs is the Source/White Light expands its love energy or just *itself* to a higher energetic vibration and thus creates a larger place of peace, love, bliss, kindness, and joy.

Thus the energetic force or love exuding from the Source increases and will continue to increase along with the energetic vibrational increase of people and the planet. As Source increases its energetic force or Source of love, this will ever so gently nudge people in the direction of love. These gentle nudges are energetic and spiritual. They will occur quite naturally because the energetic vibration from the Source/White Light is intensifying and becoming stronger in White Light, love, peace/stillness, and grace. You may begin to feel your body loosening its veils of protection, its armor of safety, and its coats of caution and become more alive in an openness that is more allowing in believing and knowing that you are already that Source.

You are already that which is love. You are already that which is of the Source – of love. Arrive then within this place of peacefulness and this place of great joy and a place you call home. Most importantly, as the vibration increases within yourself, this increases the energetic vibration of the One Source. Continue to refine your energetic vibration and in doing so the vibration from the Source will be stronger. This vibration will circulate back to the planet and back then to you. Remember, the Homo-Luminous body is the fullness of the Source.

You are the absolute purity of White Light and nothing more and nothing less. You are it! You will become attuned to your *new you*, your new way of living and being within this new form of vibration. Therefore the Homo-Luminous body is the form that is the solidity of the Source, the solidity of the God force of love. You then recognize that you are the purity of the Source of love.

This is the exact and perfect timing for you to accentuate your authentic self. It is now the time for you to draw awareness from within you and call upon this Source within your entire life. Accentuate your way of allowing the Source to glisten through you. As the Source increases its intensity, life will become easier for you and you just need to believe, know, and allow this to be true.

"It Is Time" – as Stated by the Great Masters

The old philosophers, intellectuals, spiritual leaders, inventors, artists, musicians, and other creative, talented individuals would have loved to exist during this era of great change. How excited they would have been! The great thinkers (Abraham Maslow and Einstein), musicians and composers (Bach, Beethoven, and Mozart), artists (Da Vinci, Michelangelo, and Picasso), plus many others would have agreed, "It is time." What all this means is that finally people are observing, sensing, and feeling the world differently. Our world is no longer the same and collectively the old Masters theories, philosophies, ideas concerning music and art have changed dramatically, back to where they should be, to a natural, organic place, connected to the Divine!

These great vessels or humans of channeled works of long ago would say today, if alive, "Now is the time to redesign, rewrite, reconstruct, and recreate." This essentially means that these humans all channeled messages to assist in the creation of pieces of the universe. Now is the time to recreate and update their works. Their works were required for that time period and now we require some new messages, which have been stored or contained in the energy or Spirit world ready to birth. This Crystal Collective's All Truth is therefore indicating, "It is time to recreate and rework all theories, philosophies, ideas of music, art and more."

First, let's reexamine and redesign Abraham Maslow's Hierarchy of Needs (1940):

Abraham Maslow's Original Hierarchy of Needs

Abraham Maslow's Original Hierarchy of Needs (Figure 3)

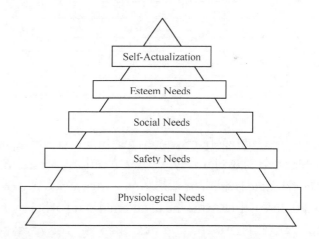

Maslow writes about self-actualization, which is at the top of his triangle illustration (see Figure 3). Self-actualization now needs to be re-positioned at the bottom of the triangle (see Figure 4). By changing the hierarchy of needs and re-positioning this to the bottom of the triangle, then human survival takes on a very different form. Thus the following will occur: the self-actualized term, which truly means *realized* or *awakened,* coincides with survival and belonging. In fact to survive means *to be awakened,* and to be awakened is defined as *to belong,* which links belonging or being in Spirit. Therefore, *to survive* means *to live.* This new hierarchy of needs called "The Awakening" may appear similar to Figure 4 illustration.

The Awakening (Figure 4)

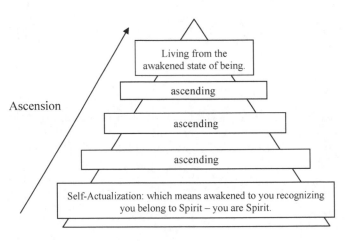

When self-actualized or awakened, then everything in life falls into place. This explains why all you require at the bottom rung of the triangle is *self-actualization*. Once awakened or self-actualized then you live from the awakened state of being or you ascend to your Higher Self. The next step is "The Awakened" triangle (see Figure 5). The bottom of this triangle illustration depicts living from the awakened state of being (which is shown on the top of Figure 4). The top of the Awakened triangle is the Homo-Luminous non-form. The form that represents the completion of shifting back to Spirit or the final ascension to the Homo-Luminous form.

See the shifting or ascension from Abraham Maslow's Hierarchy of Needs (Figure 3) to The Awakened Triangle (Figure 5). This is just one example of the many shifts occurring on the planet as we move into an awakened state of existing.

The Awakened (Figure 5)

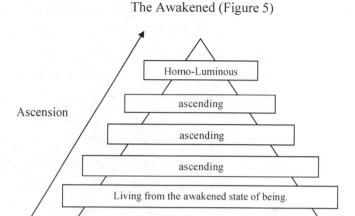

To return to the work of another great thinker – Einstein, he would have certainly enjoyed this moment in time. If he were alive today his original ideas, and theories like that of relativity, would have to shift. What this means is that his original ideas would shift today if he were alive. He wouldn't be looking so much at intellectual ideas, inventions, causes, and effect. He would instead concentrate on the rawness, the core of existence, and the Essence and how to measure this. He would no doubt also focus on the illusion of time and how to measure this illusion and also study in depth, why the sun is becoming whiter, and also why the majority of people are choosing to live in the now. Finally, his curiosity would be peaked as to why people are growing their own food and buying land. He would discover that our civilization is a time of great Awakenings and awareness.

The old Masters' artist Michelangelo and Da Vinci were aware they were simply vessels being used by Source as their talent flowed through their paintbrush or drawing utensil. They were enlightened and realized that there was a larger phenomena at work here and they also were aware that all humans had this capacity, as well.

Both Michelangelo and Da Vinci were ignored and not listened to. During their era they were considered by some historians as "mentally unbalanced," because of their enlightened views.

Today many artists, inventors, thinkers, and philosophers are beginning to view life differently, in a more Source-filled/Spirit-filled way. This depth of Spirit is moving forth as people become aware or awakened. Artists are those who are often connecting with their most inner self or core self. They begin to feel something different when they work or perform their art. This is called the *Source* or who you are. They are already in this flow. Bach, Beethoven, and Mozart all declared their music was spontaneous and just happened. They were channeling or streaming the musical information and performing the most spectacular symphonies. If they lived today, their channeled musical works would demonstrate a gently composed musical movement or piece of music named *preparation*, followed by a grand piece played in the strength and solidity of grounded musical work named *transition*. Then the final phase is the greatness of the angels singing hallelujah and this is called *metamorphosis*, thus completed by a pure ecstasy and grandeur. This full symphony piece would be called "The Original World" which shows the unfolding of the spiritual evolution in a musical sense according to the Preparation, Transition, and Metamorphosis Phases as described throughout this book.

Wouldn't it be wonderful if these great people who have crossed over many years ago were here to experience this time, which in fact they already knew about? Keep in mind, heart, and your Spirit that they are here and are watching from their spiritual or Spirit-filled dimension. They may even be called forth if you wish to access their genius of Spirit. We all have the ability to tap into *our* genius of Spirit to redesign, rewrite, reconstruct, and recreate our life.

Part III

Final Review

Summarizing the Crystals and Their Meaning

I t's important to remember that the Crystal Collectives are comprised of crystals that are the containers for not only *now* but for the next thousands of years. Spiritual evolution continues even when all beings have arrived in a place of Homo-Luminous existence. These pieces of crystallized shapes contain the *movement of stillness*. This movement is occurring during our present time. Some of these crystals have been exposed within the pages of this book and others will be exposed at a later date. A number of these crystals have specific shapes designated according to the messages they contain. Each shape represents a spiritual connection. For example, the new Mayan calendar circle represents the calendar of life. Within this crystallized circle of messages is the realization of the inner self of Spirit or Source. The circle represents the continued cycle of life, of living, of believing that all people are One, all people are functioning as One. One person loves another person thus loving Oneself; it becomes a rippling effect when we are all destined to be *One*.

The Crystal Collectives are comprised of the scribed messages of the realizations of the *now*. These realizations contain the ancient truths of the original way of being. The planet is shifting and transforming into the original. As indicated throughout this book, Crystal Collectives hold the ancient old truths or the All Truths of the original world. These are being revealed as the realizations are passed along from each person as their own truths are revealed of their own original self, which is Spirit.

The Spirit is all encompassing – all Source – to all beings as One. This spiritual evolution continues even when all beings have arrived in a place of Homo-Luminous existence. Further realizations will be revealed when ready. This preparation or readiness is being perfectly paced within the spiritual evolution. These crystallized shapes will slowly and tenderly be exposed when they need to be. All is perfectly in place.

These are grand and exciting times as the *now* awareness raises our perceptions of who we are moves us more deeply into the awakening of our Spirit. Therefore we should maintain our awakened state and only focus our energy on what is happening at this state of being awakened – that is all. Within the depths of awakening, you find the realizations of being enlightened. The deepest part of being awakened evolves in the original world. You are already *Light* – there is nothing to relight.

A Thoughtful Conclusion

As you reflect upon what you have just read, you need to realize that as one moves and shifts through life, you become life. In other words, as you shift to the original self, you then arrive back to who you really are – which is Spirit. Everything that has been written in this book is a collection of truths for the moment and during the moment it was channeled. As you continue to read and review the book contents you will discover that all information being messaged here makes sense. It all makes sense from a spiritual, soulful, emotional, energetic, and physical perspective. Once you awaken yourself or you just merely wake up, the realization sets in that something feels different.

You know that there is something big and wonderful happening in the world today. It has to be in order for things to be turned around to embrace a sense of freedom and love and for us to learn about releasing ourselves with clarity, love, passion, and compassion.

Awaken, sweet one, now is the time – a great time to be awake. Be at peace. Be your best awakened, enlightened self.

You are enlightened already! You are already Light!
You just need to awaken yourself to the Light
Being that you are. It really is this simple!

When awakened, you will discover so many
beautiful aspects of your life. You will become
that which *is* life and nothing more.
So begin today.
Rise and shine, meaning rise up to who you really
are and shine your Spirit – your Light self.
Be still.
Gently slip into the *movement of stillness.*

There is no end and there is no beginning,
just the original.
So it is.
For *Eternity*

Glossary

All Truths – The truth of living. The prophecies of the new Mayan calendar, post-2012. The All Truths were once called the mystic laws.

Awakened – When one realizes one is Spirit first and foremost but living a human experience. Realizing that you *are* peace and stillness already. You have nothing to achieve to be this stillness.

Calling – The feeling or deep knowing inside you, which gently and intuitively guides you in the direction of soul's purpose.

Channeling – Streamlining information or being a vessel for the messages to move through you.

Crystal Collectives – A collection of crystals, within the Crystal Palace, which hold the scribed All Truths messages.

Crystal Palace – That sacred place/space whereby the Crystal Collectives reside. The Crystal Palaces are beneath the sacred places on the planet. These palaces are gently situated within crystal catacombs.

Divine – Meaning Spirit/God/White Light/Source. The One Creator. The core of all humans is *the Divine*.

Ego – "Edging Grace Out." Ego is suffering pain, self-sabotage, and fear. Ego is a false identity.

Grace – That Essence of who you are: peace, love, joy, bliss.

Homo-Luminous Form – This form has no ego. It is the formless Spirit of peace, joy, love, and bliss.

Homo-Sapiens – Human form relating to hunter and gatherer.

Isness – Being your authentic self. Being true to *you* and accepting who you are.

Knowing – That place inside you that is deep believing of yourself. A true understanding without doubt.

Metamorphosis Phase – From 2019 onward is a time you *fully* metamorphose your entire way of being awakened.

Oneness – All beings coming together as One Consciousness with the new Mayan calendar representing the Oneness.

Original Self – Spirit is the original self, that part of self that is peace, love, joy, passion, and compassion.

Original World – The world of the original Spirit. The understanding that life is Spirit.

Preparation Phase—The phase is from now until the end of 2014. A time where you are discovering, defining, and exploring your true authentic self; the awakening of self.

Scribed – "One writes exactly what one hears or feels." This means the messages are moving from Source/White Light onto the Crystal Collectives. The messages are energetically printing the All Truths messages onto the Crystal Collectives.

Source/White Light/God – The One Creator. It is the *Essence* of the Spirit within each person.

Transition Phase – A time and place between 2015 and 2018 where you transition and begin to live your authentic self.

Notes

Notes

About the Author

Jacqui Derbecker is a qualified teacher, consultant, speaker, writer, and visionary. Through her passionate exploration of deeper consciousness, she teaches clients how to connect with their inner authentic self, enabling them to realize that they are the Essence of Spirit. She is the founder of The Waterview Space outside of Toronto Ont. Canada where she teaches classes, gives readings and consultations.

www.jacquiconsults.com

www.waterviewspace.com